**. . . a resource of student activities to accompany the *Write Away* handbook**

WRITE SOURCE®

GREAT SOURCE EDUCATION GROUP

a Houghton Mifflin Company
Wilmington, Massachusetts

# A Few Words About the *Write Away SkillsBook*

## Before you begin . . .

The *SkillsBook* provides you with opportunities to practice editing and proofreading skills presented in the *Write Away* handbook. The handbook contains guidelines, examples, and models to help you complete your work in the *SkillsBook.*

Each *SkillsBook* activity includes a brief introduction to the topic and examples showing how to complete that activity. You will be directed to the page numbers in the handbook for additional information and examples. The "Proofreading Activities" focus on punctuation, the mechanics of writing, usage, and spelling. The "Sentence Activities" provide practice in sentence combining and in correcting common sentence problems. The "Language Activities" highlight the parts of speech.

Many exercises end with a **KEEP GOING** activity. Its purpose is to provide follow-up work that will help you apply what you have learned in your own writing.

**Authors:** Pat Sebranek and Dave Kemper



Printed in the United States of America
International Standard Book Number: 978-0-669-48237-9 (student edition)
International Standard Book Number: 0-669-48237-4 (student edition)

9 10 -DBH- 09 08 07

International Standard Book Number: 978-0-669-48238-6 (teacher's edition)
International Standard Book Number: 0-669-48238-2 (teacher's edition)

3 4 5 6 7 8 9 10 -DBH- 09 08 07 06

# Table of Contents

## Proofreading Activities

### Using Punctuation

## Checking Mechanics



## Checking Your Spelling



## Using the Right Word

## Sentence Activities



## Language Activities

### Nouns



### Pronouns



### Verbs



### Adjectives



### Parts of Speech



## Theme Word Activities

### Theme Words

# Proofreading Activities

The activities in this section include sentences that need to be checked for punctuation, mechanics, or usage. Most of the activities also include helpful handbook references. In addition, **KEEP GOING,** which is at the end of many activities, encourages follow-up practice of certain skills.

*Name* ______________________________

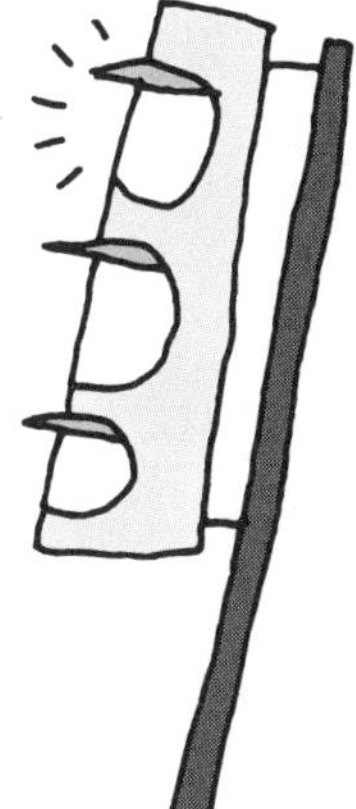

# Periods as End Punctuation

A **period** is used as a signal to stop at the end of a sentence. Put a period at the end of a telling sentence.

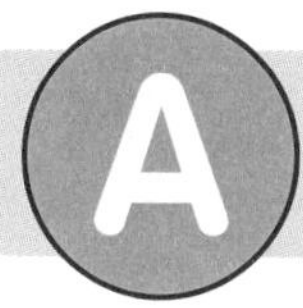

**Put periods at the ends of these telling sentences.**

1. Our class lines up at the main door __•__
2. Sometimes we make our teacher smile ______
3. We play indoors on rainy days ______
4. There are some great new books in the library ______
5. I like to write funny stories ______

**Write two telling sentences about your school.**

1. ______________________________

______________________________

2. ______________________________

______________________________

**C** **Put a period at the end of each sentence in this letter.**

October 10, 2001

Dear Aunt Fran,

I like school this year. There are 22 kids in my class A new boy sits next to me His name is Robert I think we're going to be friends I'll let you know in my next letter

Love,

Timmy

**Now answer these questions about the letter.**

**1.** How many telling sentences are in the letter? __________

**2.** How many periods are in the letter? __________

*Name* ______________________________

# Periods After Abbreviations

Use **periods** after these abbreviations: Mr., Mrs., Ms., and Dr.

Dr. Green Mrs. Linn

(**Dr.** is the abbreviation for **doctor.**)

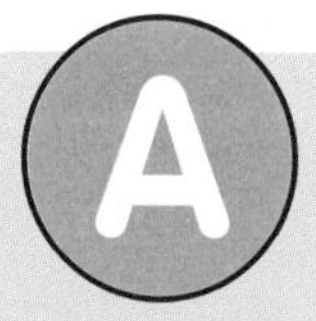

**Put periods after the abbreviations in these sentences. (Some sentences need more than one period.)**

1. Mrs. Linn is our teacher.
2. Mr and Mrs Linn have three rabbits.
3. Mr Linn gave the rabbits their names.
4. They are Ms Hop, Mr Skip, and Mrs Jump.
5. Mrs Linn took the rabbits to Dr Green for shots.
6. Dr Green said, "Those are good names!"
7. Mrs Linn told Dr Green that Mr Linn made up the names.

Write two silly names for rabbits. One name should start with Mr. and one with Mrs. Then write two sentences that use the names.

Name: Mr. ______________________________

Name: Mrs. ______________________________

1. ______________________________

______________________________

______________________________

2. ______________________________

______________________________

______________________________

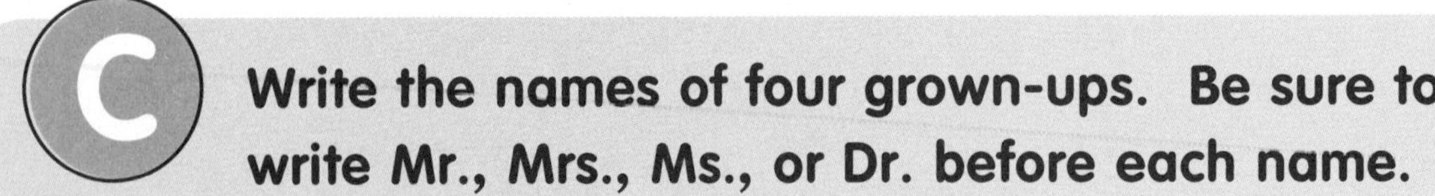

Write the names of four grown-ups. Be sure to write Mr., Mrs., Ms., or Dr. before each name.

1. ______________________________
2. ______________________________
3. ______________________________
4. ______________________________

*Name* ______________________

# Periods Between Dollars and Cents

Use a **period** (decimal point) between dollars and cents.

$1.50 $3.00 $7.95

**A** **Put periods (decimal points) between the dollars and cents in these sentences.**

1. Dan made $4.3 5 selling lemonade and cookies.
2. I paid $1 5 0 for two cookies.
3. Dan put $1 3 5 in his bank.
4. He spent $5 0 0 for two movie tickets.
5. Tickets only cost $2 5 0 on Saturday afternoon.
6. My lunch ticket cost $5 0 0 this week.
7. Ms. Bank paid $3 5 0 for lunch.
8. I saved $8 0 0 for my new bike.

**Fill in the blanks in the problems below. Remember to use decimal points correctly.**

1. \$1.00 + \$4.00 = ________
2. \$8.00 – \$2.00 = ________
3. \$3.00 + \$3.00 + \$3.00 = ________
4. \$5.00 – \$2.00 = ________
5. \$1.00 + \$2.00 + \$3.00 = ________
6. \$4.00 + \$1.00 + \$1.00 = ________

**Write each amount listed below in numerals. Remember to use decimal points correctly.**

1. One dollar and fifty cents ________
2. One dollar and twenty cents ________
3. Five dollars and ten cents ________
4. Ten dollars and sixty-nine cents ________
5. Two dollars and no cents ________
6. Six dollars and fifty cents ________

Name ___________________________

# Question Marks

Put a **question mark** after a sentence that asks a question.

What is the longest river?

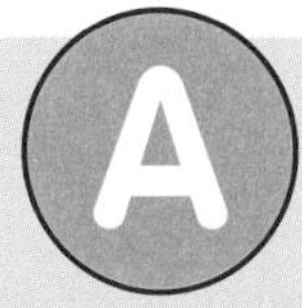


**Put a question mark after each sentence that asks a question. Put a period after each of the other sentences.**

1. The world's longest river is the Nile __.__
2. Where is the Nile ______
3. The Nile River is in Africa ______
4. Are there crocodiles in the Nile ______
5. You could jump in and find out ______
6. Are you kidding ______
7. I'd rather just ask someone ______
8. Are you afraid of crocodiles ______
9. Who wouldn't be afraid ______

**Put a period or a question mark at the end of each sentence in this paragraph.**

Lots of animals live in rivers. Of course, fish live in rivers What else lives in rivers Snails, frogs, and turtles live in and around rivers Have you heard of river otters They are very good at diving They can stay underwater for four minutes Do you know any other animals that dive

**Write two questions about rivers. Remember to use question marks!**

1. ________________________________________

2. ________________________________________

Name ____________________

# Exclamation Points

Put an **exclamation point** after an "excited" word.

Help! Yuck!

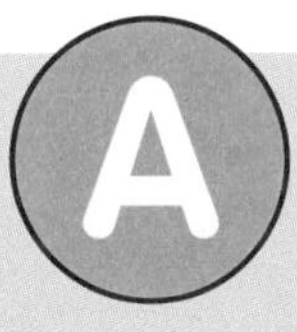

Also put an exclamation point after a sentence showing strong feeling.

Don't touch that!

**A** **Put an exclamation point after each "excited" word and after each sentence that shows strong feeling.**

1. I found a treasure map___!___
2. No way______
3. It's true______
4. Wow______
5. Let's find the treasure______
6. We'll be famous______
7. This could be dangerous______
8. I think I see a pirate______

Each of the following sentences needs an exclamation point or a question mark. Put the correct end punctuation after each sentence.

1. Look, Tom, it's a cave ______
2. It's dark ______
3. It's creepy ______
4. Did you see that ______
5. What is it ______
6. It's a bat ______
7. Wow, that's neat ______
8. Here we go ______

Imagine that you are in a dark cave. Write a sentence that ends with an exclamation point.

______________________________________________

______________________________________________

*Name* ______________________________

# End Punctuation

Use a **period (.)** after a telling sentence. Use a **question mark (?)** after a sentence that asks a question. Use an **exclamation point (!)** after a sentence that shows strong feeling.

**Put the correct end punctuation after each sentence.**

1. Dad's taking us to the ice-cream store __!__
2. Hooray! Let's have a race to the car ______
3. What flavor will Dad choose ______
4. He likes hot-fudge sundaes ______
5. What do you think Mom wants ______
6. She'll probably get frozen yogurt ______
7. What should we get ______
8. Let's get ice-cream sandwiches ______

**B** **Write a telling sentence, an asking sentence, and a sentence showing strong feeling about your favorite dessert.**

Telling Sentence: ______________________________

______________________________

Asking Sentence: ______________________________

______________________________

Strong Feeling Sentence: ______________________________

______________________________

**C** **Ask a partner a question. Write your partner's name, the question you asked, and your partner's answer.**

Partner's Name: ______________________________

Question: ______________________________

______________________________

Answer: ______________________________

______________________________

*Name* ______________________________

# End Punctuation Review

Use a **period** after a telling sentence. Use a **question mark** after a sentence that asks a question. Use an **exclamation point** after a sentence that shows strong feeling.

**Put the correct end punctuation after each sentence.**

Does this ever happen to you It's time for bed, but you're not sleepy You try to lie still You look around You just have to get up You want to get a book or a toy You try to be quiet It's hard to see in the dark You make a loud noise Someone says, "What's going on in there" Then you hear, "Get back in bed"

## B

**Draw a picture of something you like to do after school.**

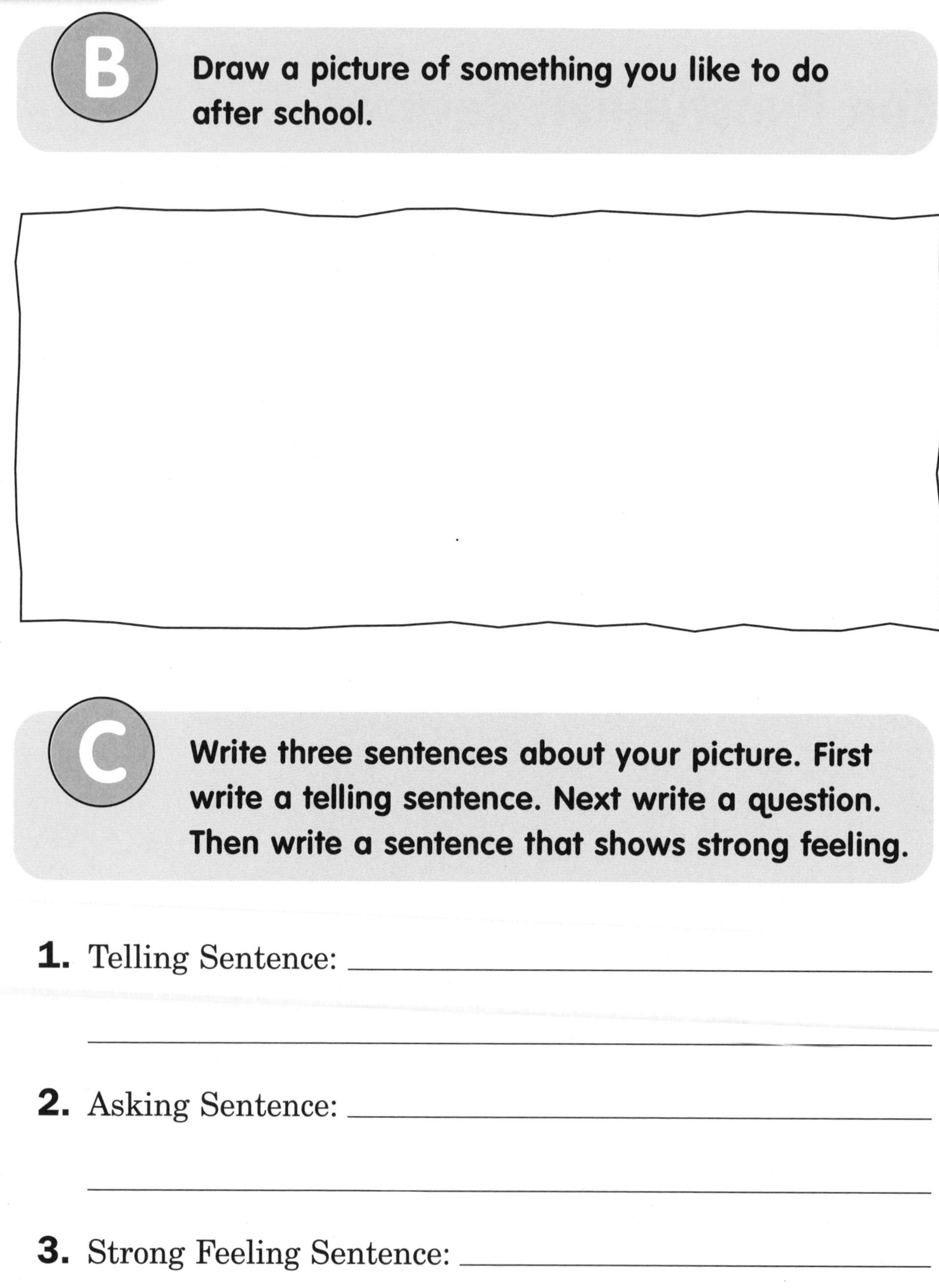

## C

**Write three sentences about your picture. First write a telling sentence. Next write a question. Then write a sentence that shows strong feeling.**

**1.** Telling Sentence: ____________________

____________________

**2.** Asking Sentence: ____________________

____________________

**3.** Strong Feeling Sentence: ____________________

____________________

Name ______________________________

# Comma Between a City and a State

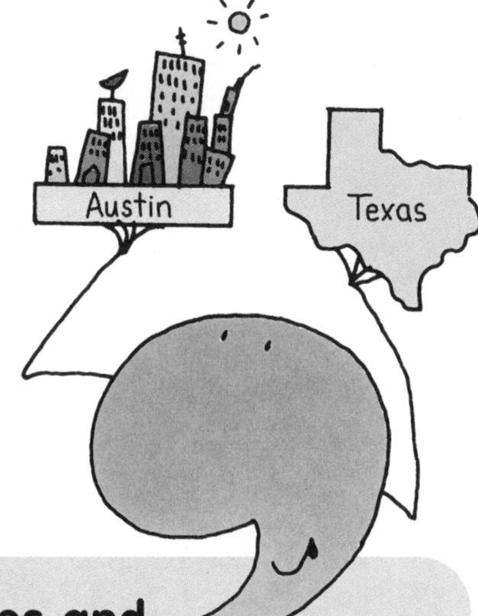


Put a **comma** between the name of a city and a state.

Austin, Texas     Salem, Oregon

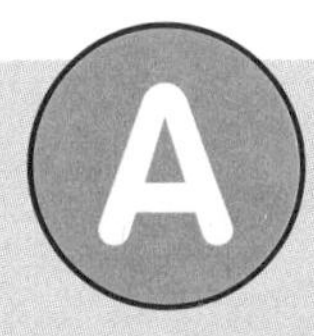

**Put commas between the cities and states below.**

1. Calumet, Michigan
2. Casper Wyoming
3. Williamsburg Virginia
4. Portland Maine
5. Dallas Texas
6. Dayton Ohio

**Write the names of three cities and states shown on the United States map on page 319 in your handbook. Be sure to put a comma between the name of the city and the state.**

1. ______________________________
2. ______________________________
3. ______________________________

**Draw a picture of a place in your city or town. Beneath your drawing, write sentences about your picture.**

I live in ________________________________

________________________________

________________________________

________________________________

________________________________

Name ______________________________

# Comma Between the Day and the Year

Put a **comma** between the day and the year.

January 17, 2004
November 12, 2004

| December 2004 | | | | | | |
|---|---|---|---|---|---|---|
| S | M | T | W | T | F | S |
| | | | 1 | 2 | 3 | 4 |
| 5 | 6 | 7 | 8 | 9 | 10 | 11 |
| (12) | 13 | 14 | 15 | 16 | 17 | 18 |
| 19 | 20 | 21 | 22 | 23 | 24 | ◇25 |
| 26 | 27 | 28 | 29 | 30 | 31 | |

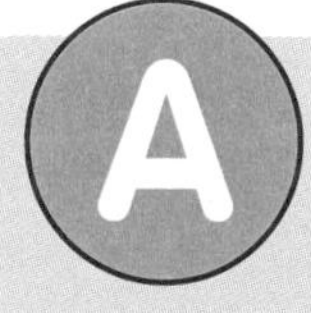


**Look at the calendar on this page. Then write the correct month, day, and year.**

1. Write the date that is circled.

   December 12, 2004
   ______________________________

2. Write the date that has a diamond around it.

   ______________________________

3. Write the date for the last day of the month.

   ______________________________

4. Write the date for the first Monday of the month.

   ______________________________

**Write the dates for the following days. Be sure to include the month, day, and year. The months are listed on page 260 in your handbook.**

**1.** Your next birthday:

______________________________

**2.** Today:

______________________________

**3.** Tomorrow:

______________________________

**Write a true or make-believe sentence about the day you were born. Include the date of your birth in your sentence.**

______________________________

______________________________

______________________________

______________________________

______________________________

Name ______________________

# Commas in Letters

Put **commas** after the greeting and the closing of a letter.

Dear Grandpa Joe, ← **greeting**

I love my new fishing rod! Thank you! Can we go fishing soon? I hope so!

Love,

Ben ↖ **closing**

**A** **Put commas where they belong in these letters.**

May 10, 2001

Dear Ben

Ask your mom when your family is coming to Florida. Then we can go fishing.

Love

Grandpa Joe

May 18, 2001

Dear Grandpa Joe

We are coming to see you on June 24 after school is out. I can't wait! My tackle box is ready.

Love

Ben

**B** **Put commas in Grandpa's letter. Then pretend you are Ben. Write what you would say in your next letter to Grandpa Joe. Be sure to put commas in the right places.**

May 24, 2001

Dear Ben

I will be seeing you in one month! We'll camp out in a tent. We'll have a campfire.

Love

Grandpa Joe

____________________
(Date)

____________________
(Greeting)

________________________________________

________________________________________

____________________
(Closing)

____________________
(Signature)

Name ______________________________

# Commas in Big Numbers

Use **commas** to keep big numbers clear.

I said there were 10,000 ants at the picnic.

Mr. Dell said there were only 8,500.

**Put a comma where it is needed in each number.**

1. Joey's little brother asks the same question 2 0 0 0 times.
2. Mrs. Roundtree has a book with 1 1 1 7 pages.
3. A crowd of 4 5 0 0 people watched the fireworks.
4. About 1 0 0 0 0 mosquitoes were there, too.
5. Uncle Harry always says, "That's the $6 4 0 0 0 question!"
6. The deepest part of the Pacific Ocean is 3 6 1 9 8 feet deep.
7. Mount McKinley is 2 0 3 2 0 feet above sea level.
8. Angel Falls is 3 2 1 2 feet high.

**Open your handbook to page 321. Write a sentence that answers each question. Make sure to use commas correctly in your numbers.**

**1.** How long is the Mississippi River?

______________________________________________

**2.** How high is Mt. McKinley?

______________________________________________

______________________________________________

**3.** How big is the largest desert in the United States?

______________________________________________

**4.** How big is the largest lake?

______________________________________________

**5.** How big is the smallest state?

______________________________________________

**Draw a picture of a mountain. Use your own paper. On your drawing, write a sentence telling how high your mountain is.**

*Name* ______________________________

# Commas Between Words in a Series

Put **commas** between words in a series.

The five senses are sight, hearing, taste, smell, and touch.

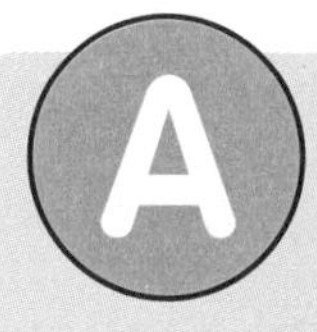

**Put commas where they are needed in these sentences.**

1. Most foods taste sweet, sour, or salty.
2. Smell sight and taste help us enjoy food.
3. Almost everybody likes candy cookies and cake.
4. Pizza brownies and roses smell good.
5. Cats can see only black white and gray.
6. Dogs cats and bats hear all kinds of sounds.
7. Sounds can be loud soft or just right.
8. Teddy bears are soft cuddly and fuzzy.

## B List three or four things in each category below.

| My Favorite **Tastes** | My Favorite **Smells** | My Favorite **Sounds** |
| --- | --- | --- |
| | | |
| | | |
| | | |
| | | |
| | | |

## C Finish the sentences below using words from your lists. Remember to use commas between words in a series.

**1.** My favorite tastes are ______________________________

______________________ and ______________________ .

**2.** My favorite smells are ______________________________

______________________ and ______________________ .

**3.** My favorite sounds are ______________________________

______________________ and ______________________ .

*Name* ______________________________

# Commas to Set Off a Speaker's Words

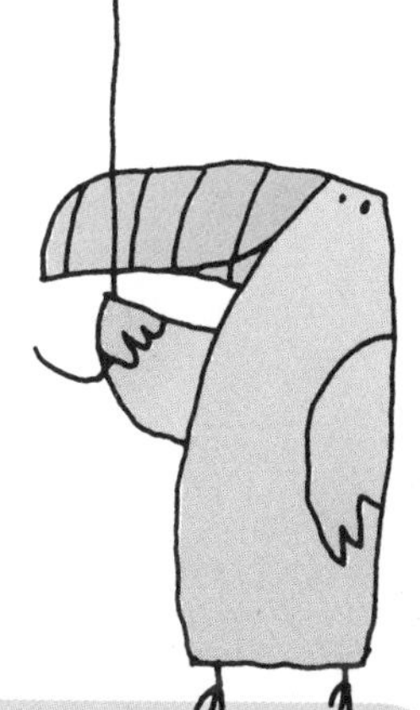

When you write a speaker's exact words, you may tell who is speaking at the **beginning** of the sentence, or at the **end** of the sentence.

Mr. Kent said, "Kari, you may begin your report."

"My report is on birds," Kari said.

**Put commas where they are needed in these sentences.**

"Many birds migrate in the winter," Kari said.

Darrin asked "What does *migrate* mean?"

"Migrate means that some birds go to a new place in winter" Kari answered. She added "Birds migrate to find food and water."

"That's very interesting" said Mr. Kent.

**B** Write questions that Bill and Regina might ask about birds and migration. Use question marks and commas correctly.

Bill asked "________________________________________

________________________________________________

________________________________________________"

Regina asked "______________________________________

________________________________________________

________________________________________________"

KEEP GOING

List three places you would like to migrate (travel) to.

1. ______________________________________________

2. ______________________________________________

3. ______________________________________________

*Name* ______________________________

# Comma Review

This activity reviews comma uses you have learned.

**Put a comma between the names of the cities and the states in these sentences.**

1. You can see mountains from Portland Oregon.
2. The James River goes through Richmond Virginia.
3. El Paso Texas, is near Mexico.
4. Sitka Alaska, is on the Pacific Ocean.
5. Hilo Hawaii, is part of an island.

**Put a comma between the day and the year in these sentences.**

1. George Washington was born February 22 1732.
2. The first nickel was made on May 16 1866.
3. On February 7 1867, Laura Ingalls Wilder was born.
4. The astronaut Sally Ride was born May 26 1951.

## C Put commas between words in a series in these sentences.

1. Red orange yellow and green are rainbow colors.
2. My uncle aunt and cousin live in Michigan.
3. Jonathan likes snowboarding sledding and skiing.
4. My family has two cats one dog and a turtle.
5. I send letters notes and e-mail messages.

## D Put commas where they are needed.

Maggie asked "What kind of seashell is that?"

"It's a heart cockle" Molly said. "If you put two together, they form a heart."

"Amazing!" Maggie added. "What's this one?"

"It's called a turkey wing" Molly answered.

"That's a perfect name! It looks just like one" said Maggie.

*Name* ______________________________

# Making Contractions

A **contraction** turns two words into one word. To make a contraction, put an apostrophe where one or more letters are left out.

| Two Words | Contraction |
|---|---|
| does not | doesn't |
| he will | he'll |

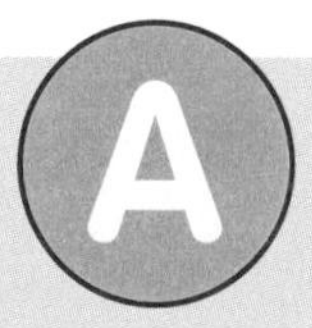

**In the second column, cross out the letters that are left out of the contraction in the first column.**

| | Contraction | Two Words |
|---|---|---|
| **1.** | I'm | I am |
| **2.** | she'll | she will |
| **3.** | he's | he is |
| **4.** | they're | they are |
| **5.** | he'd | he would |
| **6.** | hasn't | has not |
| **7.** | we'll | we will |
| **8.** | shouldn't | should not |

## B Make contractions from the words below. Remember to use an apostrophe each time!

1. do not ______________________
2. that is ______________________
3. cannot ______________________
4. I have ______________________

## C On each blank below, write the contraction for the words in parentheses.

1. ______________________ going to make a mask.
   (I am)
2. ______________________ make it out of a paper bag.
   (I will)
3. ______________________ going to be a scary mask.
   (It is)
4. Dad ______________________ know I am making it.
   (does not)

*Name* ______________________________

# Apostrophes in Contractions

A **contraction** turns two words (or one longer word) into one word. To make a contraction, put an apostrophe where one or more letters are left out.

| Two Words | Contraction |
|---|---|
| she will | she'll |

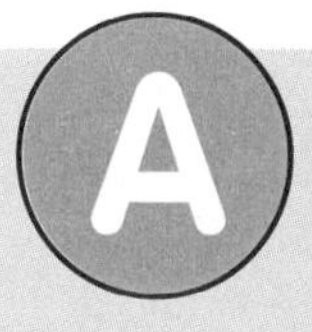

**In each sentence, underline the contraction. Then write the word or words the contraction stands for. The first one has been done for you.**

1. "Peter didn't obey Mom," said Flopsy. did not
2. "You can't go to the ball," she told Cinderella. ______________
3. "You wouldn't help me," said the Little Red Hen. ______________
4. "I couldn't sleep in that bumpy bed," said the princess. ______________
5. The wolf said, "I'll blow your house down." ______________
6. "I'm a real boy!" shouted Pinocchio. ______________

**Write the two words that each contraction stands for. The first one has been done for you.**

1. doesn't does not
2. hasn't ______
3. he's ______
4. I've ______
5. isn't ______
6. it's ______
7. we're ______
8. you'll ______

**Write a sentence using one of the contractions above.**

______

______

______

*Name* ________________________________

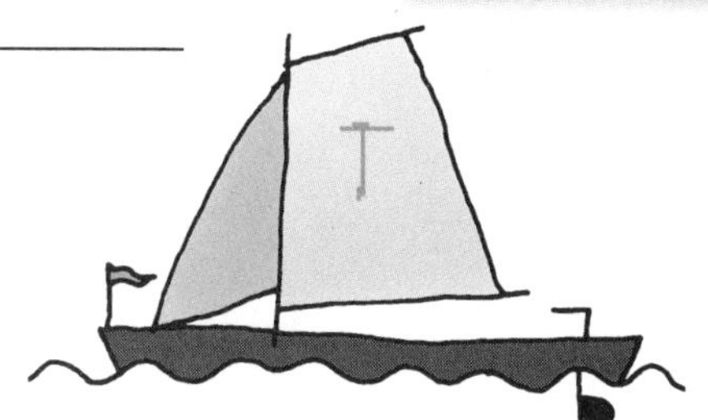

# Apostrophes to Show Ownership

Add an **apostrophe** and an **"s"** to a word to show ownership.

Tom has a boat. It is Tom's boat.

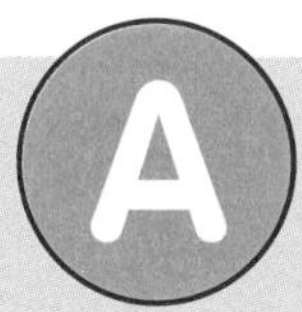

**Each phrase below shows ownership. Draw a picture in each box.**

| | |
|---|---|
| **the cat's rug** | **the bird's nest** |
| **Susan's jump rope** | **my mother's hat** |

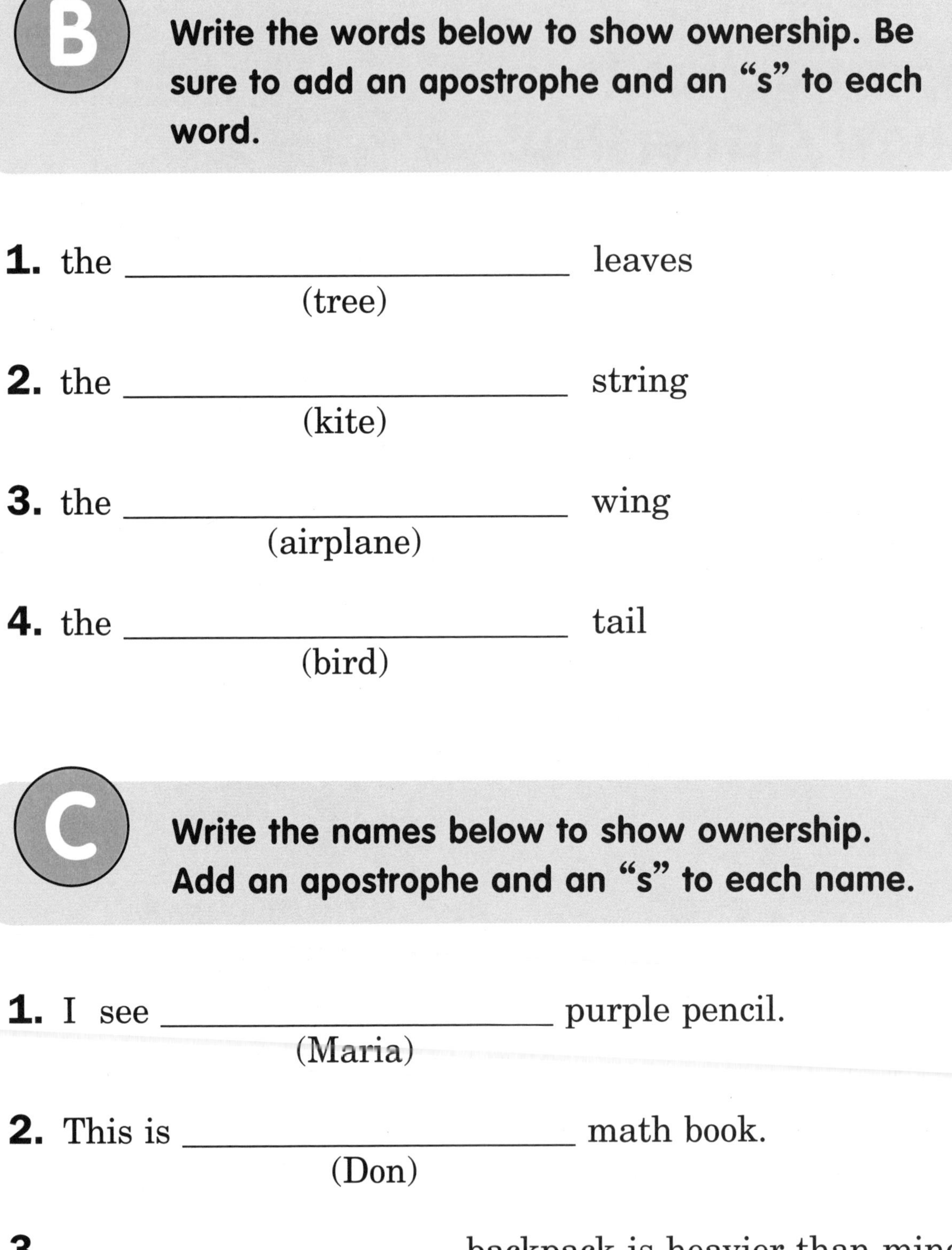

## B

**Write the words below to show ownership. Be sure to add an apostrophe and an "s" to each word.**

**1.** the ______________________ leaves
(tree)

**2.** the ______________________ string
(kite)

**3.** the ______________________ wing
(airplane)

**4.** the ______________________ tail
(bird)

## C

**Write the names below to show ownership. Add an apostrophe and an "s" to each name.**

**1.** I see ______________________ purple pencil.
(Maria)

**2.** This is ______________________ math book.
(Don)

**3.** ______________________ backpack is heavier than mine.
(Jane)

**4.** ______________________ idea notebook is on the desk.
(Sol)

Name ______________________

# Quotation Marks Before and After a Speaker's Words

Comic strips make it easy to tell who is speaking. They use speech balloons. Here Mom and Steve are talking about dinner.

When you write sentences, you use **quotation marks** to show the speaker's exact words.

Steve asked, "Mom, can we make pizza for dinner?"

"That sounds really good to me," Mom said.

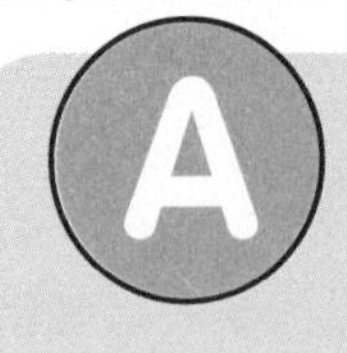

**A** **Read the speech balloons. Then write the sentences below. Put quotation marks where they are needed.**



Steve asked, ______________________________

______________________________

Mom answered, ______________________________

______________________________



Steve asked, ______________________________

______________________________

Mom said, ______________________________

______________________________

Name ______________________________

# Quotation Marks for Titles

Put **quotation marks** around the titles of stories and poems.

**a story** — "Goldilocks"

**a poem** — "Monday Morning Good"

**Put quotation marks around the titles in these sentences.**

1. "The Tortoise and the Hare" is a fable.
2. The Ugly Duckling is my favorite fairy tale.
3. Eletelephony is a poem that makes me laugh.
4. I like the poem Beans, Beans, Beans.
5. We read the fable The Lion and the Mouse.
6. We read the poem Oodles of Noodles.
7. Did you read Rumpelstiltskin yet?

**Use your handbook to help you fill in each blank with the correct title. Make sure to use quotation marks correctly.**

1. The fable ________________________________________ is on page 131.

2. A shape poem called ______________________________ is on page 151.

3. An add-on story called ______________________________ is found on page 127.

4. ______________________________ is the all-about-me story on page 77.

5. A poem called ________________________ is on page 143.

**Write a sentence about a poem or a story you like. Give the title and use quotation marks correctly.**

____________________________________________________________

____________________________________________________________

____________________________________________________________

Name ______________________________

# Underlining Titles

**Underline** the titles of books and magazines.

**a book** — Onion Sundaes

**a magazine** — 3, 2, 1 Contact

**A** **Underline the titles in the following sentences.**

1. My sister's favorite book is Pocahontas.
2. My grandmother has a book called Mrs. Bird.
3. Kids Discover is a magazine for kids.
4. The title of our handbook is Write Away.
5. Ranger Rick is a nature magazine for kids.
6. I just read Ira Sleeps Over by Bernard Waber.
7. My dad reads National Geographic every month.
8. Our teacher is reading All About Sam to us.

## B Complete the following sentences. Remember to underline the titles.

**1.** My favorite book is ______________________________

______________________________________________.

**2.** My favorite magazine is __________________________

______________________________________________.

**3.** The title of the last book I read is ________________

______________________________________________.

**Draw a cover for one of your favorite books. Write the book title on your cover.**

*Name* ______________________________

# Punctuation Review

This review covers punctuation marks you have learned.

**Fill in each list below. Use funny or real names.**

| Cat Names | City Names | Food Names |
| --- | --- | --- |
| 1. Buddy | 1. ______ | 1. ______ |
| 2. ______ | 2. ______ | 2. ______ |
| 3. ______ | 3. ______ | 3. ______ |

**B** **Use your lists to write some funny sentences.**

**1.** Write a **telling sentence** about three cats.

______________________________

______________________________

**2.** Write an **asking sentence** about three cities.

______________________________

______________________________

3. Write an **exciting sentence** about three foods.

______________________________________________

______________________________________________

## C Write contractions for the words below.

1. did not ______________
2. you are ______________
3. I am ______________
4. it is ______________
5. they will ______________
6. cannot ______________
7. we have ______________
8. has not ______________
9. is not ______________
10. she is ______________

## D Fill in each blank with a word that shows ownership.

1. The dog has a ball. It is the ______________ ball.
2. Alisha has a computer. It is ______________ computer.
3. Our teacher has a bike. It is our ______________ bike.
4. Barry has a pet bird. It is ______________ pet bird.

*Name* ______________________________

# Capital Letters to Begin Sentences

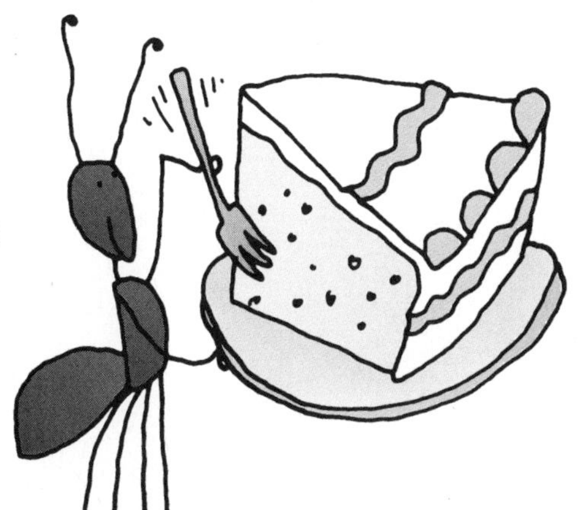

Always use a **capital letter** for the first word in a sentence.

We go to the park in the summer.

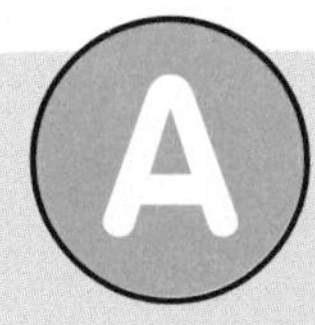


**Begin each of the following sentences with a capital letter.**

1. one day we had a picnic.
2. aunt Jill brought a big bowl of fruit salad.
3. grandma made lemonade and a chocolate cake.
4. we had sub sandwiches and taco chips.
5. all the kids played softball before lunch.
6. after the game everyone drank lemonade.
7. grandma's cake was the best part of the picnic.
8. the ants liked it, too.

**B** **Put a capital letter at the beginning of each sentence. Put a period at the end of each sentence.**

There's a swimming pool at our park. sometimes we go there for a swim i learned how to swim last year now I can go in the deep end of the pool my little sister can't swim yet she stays in the shallow end maybe I'll teach her how to swim

**Write two sentences about things you like to do in the summer. Remember to use capital letters and periods.**

**1.** ______________________________

______________________________

**2.** ______________________________

______________________________

Name ______________________________

# Capital Letter for a Speaker's First Word

Use a **capital letter** for a speaker's first word.

He asked, "Can you guess what this is?"

**Add capital letters where they are needed.**

1. Our teacher asked, "do you know the story of the blind men and the elephant?"
2. "i do," said Jasmine. "one man feels the elephant's trunk. he thinks an elephant is like a big snake."
3. "another man feels the ear," Kerry added. "he thinks an elephant is like a big fan."
4. Jasmine said, "another man feels the leg. he thinks an elephant is like a tree trunk."
5. Then Ms. Tyler asked, "how could they know the truth?"
6. Kerry said, "they could work and talk together."

## B Add capital letters where they are needed.

1. Ms. Tyler said, “that’s right, Kerry.”
2. She asked, “when do you like to work together?”
3. Kerry answered, “i like working together to perform plays.”
4. Jasmine added, “that’s something one person can’t do alone.”

**Complete this sentence telling what the elephant thinks about the blind men.**

The elephant said, “ ______________________________

__________________________________________.”

Name ______________________________

# Capital Letters for Names and Titles

Use **capital letters** for people's names and titles.

Mr. Thomas lives in a little house.
Mrs. Thomas lives there, too.

**A** **Add capital letters where they are needed.**

1. Our class helper is mrs. cantu.
2. The school nurse is mr. thomas.
3. Yesterday, will and I went to see dr. paula.
4. I asked ms. diGiaimo to read me a story.
5. Mr. and mrs. chang picked us up at camp.
6. Tomorrow, ms. banks and sally are coming over.
7. Our dentist is dr. villa.
8. After school, mr. collins helps us cross the street.

Draw a picture or paste a photo of your favorite grown-up.

Write two sentences telling why you like this grown-up. Make sure to use the grown-up's title and name each time.

1. ______________________________

______________________________

2. ______________________________

______________________________

*Name* ______________________________

# Capital Letter for "I"

Use a **capital letter** for the word "I."

I have curly red hair.
Cory and I like to tap-dance.

**Write the word "I" in each of these sentences.**

1. Jimmy and ___I___ are friends.
2. Sometimes ______ go to his house.
3. ______ ride there on my bike.
4. Sometimes Jimmy and ______ play at the park.

**Write two sentences of your own using the word "I."**

1. ______________________________________________

______________________________________________

2. ______________________________________________

______________________________________________

Draw a picture of yourself in the box below. Then write three sentences about yourself. Use the word "I" in each sentence.

1. ______________________________

______________________________

2. ______________________________

______________________________

3. ______________________________

______________________________

Name ___

# Capital Letters for Book Titles

Most words in book titles begin with **capital letters.**

➘ Town Mouse, Country Mouse

Some words do not begin with capital letters (unless they are the first or last word of a title). Here are some examples:

a an the and but of

to with by for on

**Write the four underlined book titles correctly on the lines below.**

I went to the library yesterday. I found some wonderful books! I checked out my great-aunt arizona, boxcar children, the three sillies, and the new kid on the block.

1. My Great-Aunt Arizona
2. ___
3. ___
4. ___

## B Interview yourself! Write down the titles of your favorite book and magazine.

Book: ______________________________

Magazine: ______________________________

**Write a note telling someone about your favorite book or magazine.**

Dear ____________________ ,

______________________________

______________________________

______________________________

______________________________

______________________________

Your friend,

______________________

Name ______________________________

# Capital Letters for Days of the Week

Use **capital letters** for days of the week.

Sunday Wednesday

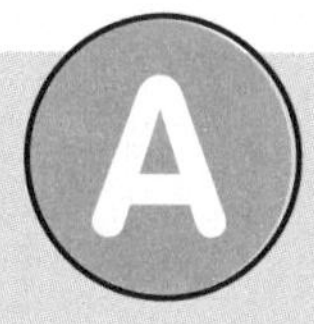

**A** **Answer the questions below. Remember to use capital letters correctly.**

1. Which day comes after Saturday? Sunday
2. Which day is between Tuesday and Thursday?

   ______________________________
3. Which day begins with the letter "F"? ______________
4. Which day is the first day of the school week?

   ______________________________
5. Which day is your least favorite day? ______________
6. Which day is your favorite day? ______________
7. Which day comes before Friday? ______________

**B** Put the days of the week in the correct order, starting with Sunday.

Thursday Sunday Tuesday Monday

Friday Wednesday Saturday

1. ______________________
2. ______________________
3. ______________________
4. ______________________
5. ______________________
6. ______________________
7. ______________________

Write a sentence about your favorite day of the week.

______________________________________________

______________________________________________

______________________________________________

*Name* ________________________________

# Capital Letters for Months of the Year 1

Use **capital letters** for the months of the year.

February        May

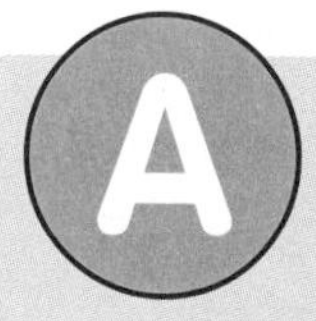

**Use capital letters for the months in these sentences.**

1. The first day of spring is in march.
2. The first day of summer is in june.
3. The first day of fall is in september.
4. The first day of winter is in december.
5. The first month of the year is january.
6. The shortest month is february.
7. Usually july and august are the hottest months.
8. april showers bring spring flowers.

**Here are three more months. Write each month correctly.**

may ______________________

october ______________________

november ______________________

**KEEP GOING** **Write one sentence about each month above.**

1. ______________________

______________________

______________________

2. ______________________

______________________

______________________

3. ______________________

______________________

______________________

*Name* ______________________________

# Capital Letters for Months of the Year 2

Use **capital letters** for the months of the year.

**Read the sentences below. Write the month correctly on the line after each sentence.**

1. Handwriting Day is the 12th of january. January
2. Groundhog Day is in february. ____________
3. Arbor Day is in april. ____________
4. Memorial Day is the last Monday in may. ____________
5. My birthday is in june. ____________
6. Halfway Day is the second of july. ____________
7. Labor Day is in september. ____________
8. Fire Prevention Week is during october. ____________
9. Thanksgiving Day is in november. ____________

Unscramble these months and write them correctly on the lines below. Remember to use a capital letter for the first letter!

1. uejn ___June___
2. gsatuu ______
3. hamrc ______
4. yrjnuaa ______
5. larip ______
6. yma ______
7. tbreoco ______
8. eeedmbcr ______
9. eyfbarru ______
10. ljuy ______
11. ervbnome ______
12. tpbreesme ______

*Name* ________________________________________

# Capital Letters for Holidays

Use **capital letters** for the names of holidays.

Father's Day Thanksgiving Day

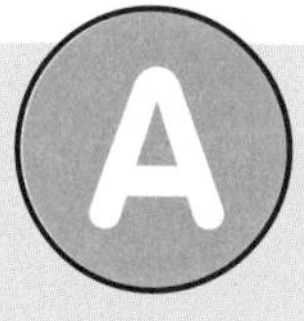

**Use capital letters for the holidays in these sentences. ("Day" is part of many holiday names.)**

1. new year's day is in January.
2. We made cards for valentine's day.
3. We celebrate presidents' day in February.
4. mother's day and memorial day are always in May.
5. One holiday in June is flag day.
6. July 4 is independence day.
7. The first Monday in September is labor day.
8. The second Monday in October is columbus day.

## B Write the names of three holidays that were not found in the sentences on page 61.

1. ______________________________

2. ______________________________

3. ______________________________

Now use the names of those three holidays in sentences.

1. ______________________________

______________________________

______________________________

2. ______________________________

______________________________

______________________________

3. ______________________________

______________________________

______________________________

Name ______________________________

# Capital Letters for Names of Places

Use a **capital letter** for the name of a city, a state, or a country.

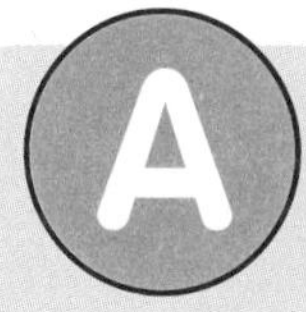

| City | State | Country |
|---|---|---|
| Carson City | Nevada | France |
| Rome | Iowa | Chad |

**A** **Write the city, state, or country correctly in the following sentences.**

1. Make Way for Ducklings takes place in the city of boston. Boston
2. The Everglades are in florida. ____________
3. My grandma is from ireland. ____________
4. Mt. Fuji is in japan. ____________
5. The Sears Tower is in chicago. ____________
6. The Peach State is georgia. ____________
7. The capital of Alaska is juneau. ____________

## B Use the map on page 319 of your handbook to answer these questions.

**1.** Which two states have "South" in their names?

______________________

______________________

**2.** Which two states begin with the letter "K"?

______________________

______________________

**3.** Which three states have only four letters in their names?

______________________

______________________

______________________

**4.** Which state do you live in?

______________________

**5.** Name a state that is near your home state.

______________________

**6.** Which state has four eyes (i's) but cannot see?

______________________

Name ______________________________

# Capital Letters Review

This activity reviews some of the different ways to use **capital letters**.

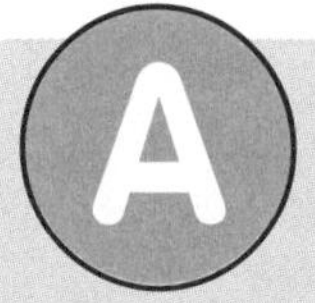

**Put capital letters where they are needed. (There are 19 in all.) Watch for these things:**

- **first word in a sentence,**
- **names and titles of people, and**
- **names of cities, states, and countries.**

our class is studying rivers. mr. banks read a book to us about the nashua river. the book was written by lynne cherry. we also learned about the nile river in africa. it is the longest river in the world. ms. johnson visited our class she went down the amazon river on a raft! she showed slides of her trip.

Put capital letters where they are needed. (There are 11 in all.) Watch for these things:

* a speaker's first word,
* names of days and months, and
* names of holidays.

1. Joel said, "my favorite day is sunday. What's yours?"
2. "sunday is my favorite day, too," I answered.
3. "what's your favorite month?" Molly asked.
4. I said, "my favorite month is july, because it's summer, and that's when I was born."
5. Molly said, "my favorite month is december, because that's when we celebrate hanukkah."
6. "that's when we celebrate christmas," I said.

Put capital letters where they are needed in these titles.

1. the tigger movie
2. the fox and the hound

Name ______________________________

# Plurals

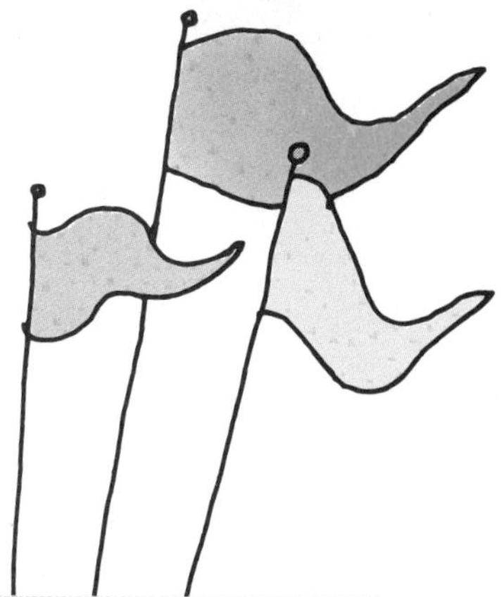

**Plural** means more than one. For most nouns, make the plurals by adding **"s."**

desk → desks window → windows

**Here is a list of things that may be in your classroom. Write the plural forms of the nouns. Then add two of your own examples.**

1. flag ______ flags ______
2. table ______________
3. eraser ______________
4. pencil ______________
5. book ______________
6. marker ______________
7. door ______________
8. ruler ______________
9. ______________ ______________
10. ______________ ______________

**Fill in the blanks by changing the singular word under the line into a plural word.**

There are 16 ________________ and 10 ________________
(girl) (boy)
in my class this year. We have one teacher and two

__________________. There are three learning
(helper)

__________________ in the classroom. In the reading center
(center)

there are lots of __________________. The art center has
(magazine)

some very bright __________________. In the writing center
(marker)

there's a whole box of __________________ and many different
(pencil)

__________________ of paper. I love my classroom!
(kind)

KEEP GOING

**Write a sentence telling how many boys and girls there are in your class.**

______________________________________________________________

______________________________________________________________

______________________________________________________________

*Name* ______________________________

# Plurals Using "s" and "es" 1

For most nouns, make the **plurals** by adding **"s."**

| | |
|---|---|
| one bird | two birds |
| a bike | four bikes |

For some nouns, you need to do more. Add **"es"** to words that end in ***sh***, ***ch***, ***s***, or ***x***.

| | |
|---|---|
| a bush | some bushes |
| one box | two boxes |

**Write the plurals of the following nouns. It's easy—just add "s."**

| | | | |
|---|---|---|---|
| **1.** bug | bugs | **6.** dog | ________ |
| **2.** river | ________ | **7.** house | ________ |
| **3.** eye | ________ | **8.** desk | ________ |
| **4.** ear | ________ | **9.** tree | ________ |
| **5.** sister | ________ | **10.** lake | ________ |

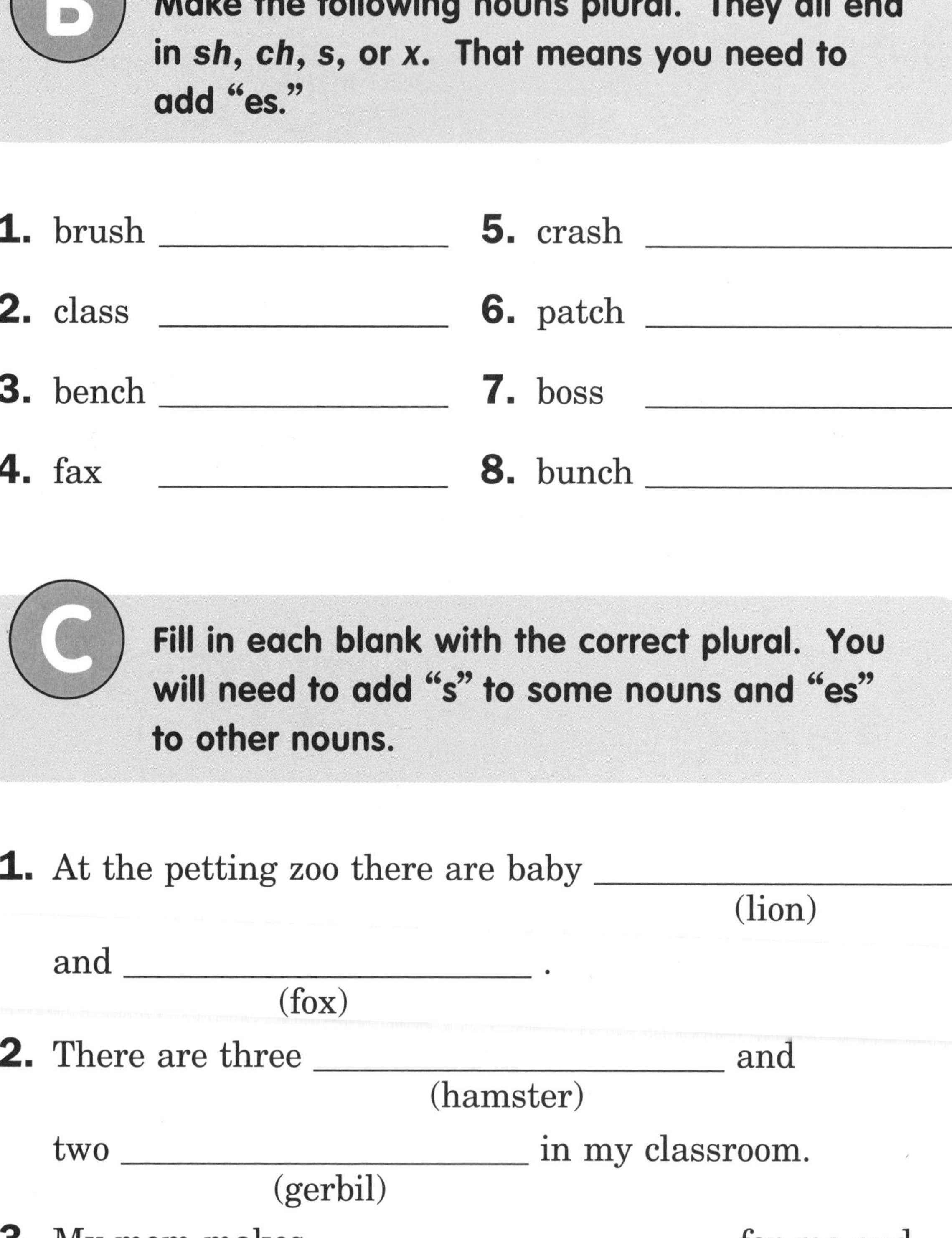

**B** **Make the following nouns plural. They all end in *sh*, *ch*, *s*, or *x*. That means you need to add "es."**

**1.** brush ____________________ **5.** crash ____________________

**2.** class ____________________ **6.** patch ____________________

**3.** bench ____________________ **7.** boss ____________________

**4.** fax ____________________ **8.** bunch ____________________

**C** **Fill in each blank with the correct plural. You will need to add "s" to some nouns and "es" to other nouns.**

**1.** At the petting zoo there are baby ____________________ (lion) and ____________________ (fox).

**2.** There are three ____________________ (hamster) and two ____________________ (gerbil) in my classroom.

**3.** My mom makes ____________________ (lunch) for me and my two ____________________ (brother).

*Name* ______________________________

# Plurals Using "s" and "es" 2

Make the **plurals** of most nouns by adding **"s."**

one snack　　　two snacks

For nouns that end in ***sh***, ***ch***, ***s***, or ***x***, add **"es"** to make the plurals.

one lunch　　　two lunches

**Write the plurals of the following nouns. Add "s" or "es."**

1. apple ______________
2. carrot ______________

3. dish ______________

4. glass ______________

5. spoon ______________
6. box ______________
7. peach ______________
8. sandwich ______________
9. raisin ______________
10. cookie ______________

**Draw a funny lunchbox on your own paper. Include some of the things you just listed.**

Name ______________________________

# Words That Change to Make Plurals

A few nouns make their **plurals** by changing letters and words. Here are some examples:

child - **children** ↙
foot - **feet**
goose - **geese**
knife - **knives**
man - **men**
mouse - **mice**
wife - **wives**
woman - **women**
wolf - **wolves**

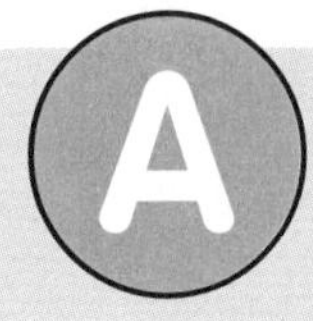

**Fill in each blank with the correct plural from the nouns above.**

1. There's a song about three blind ___mice___ .
2. You clap with your hands and walk with your __________ .
3. Set the table with ______________, forks, and spoons.
4. Ducks and ______________ like to swim in ponds.
5. Sheep need to be protected from ______________ .
6. Cartoons are for ______________, but______________ and ______________ watch them, too.
7. Husbands have ______________ .

*Name* ______________________________

# Plurals of Words That End in "y" 1

Here are two rules for making **plurals** of nouns ending in **"y"**:

**Rule 1** If there is a vowel right before the **"y,"** just add **"s."**

turkey turkeys

**Rule 2** If there is a consonant right before the **"y,"** change the **"y"** to **"i"** and add **"es."**

puppy puppies

**Make the following nouns plural using rule 1 or rule 2.**

**1.** story stories

**2.** candy ______________________________

**3.** donkey ______________________________

**4.** key ______________________________

**5.** baby ______________________________

**6.** day ______________________________

**B** Here are some more nouns that end in "y." Write their plurals. Be sure to check the letter before the "y."

1. monkey ________
2. lady ________
3. fly ________
4. toy ________
5. kitty ________
6. battery ________
7. holiday ________
8. bay ________

Circle three of the plurals you just made. Use each one in a sentence.

1. ________________________________________

________________________________________

2. ________________________________________

________________________________________

3. ________________________________________

________________________________________

Name ________________________________

# Plurals of Words That End in "y" 2

Some words end with a consonant and "**y**." To make their plurals, change "**y**" to "**i**" and add "**es**."

one baby → two babies

one story → two stories

**Write the plurals of the following nouns. Use the rule you just learned.**

1. cherry ______________
2. kitty ______________
3. party ______________
4. French fry ______________
5. guppy ______________
6. bunny ______________
7. pony ______________
8. puppy ______________
9. country ______________
10. worry ______________

**On your own paper, draw a picture of some of the animals you just listed.**

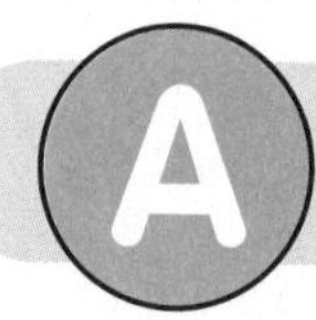

Name ______________________________

# Plurals Review

This activity reviews making **plurals**.

**A** **Make these nouns plural by adding "s" or "es."**

1. glass glasses
2. brush ________
3. frog ________
4. bus ________
5. dress ________
6. worm ________

**B** **Make these nouns plural by adding "s" or changing "y" to "i" and adding "es."**

1. monkey ________
2. puppy ________
3. day ________
4. turkey ________
5. toy ________
6. cherry ________

**C** **Change these words to make them plural.**

1. mouse ________
2. foot ________
3. woman ________
4. knife ________

*Name* ______________________________

# Abbreviations

Put a **period** after a person's title.

**Mr.** **Mrs.** **Ms.** **Dr.**

Ms. Walters Mr. Johnson

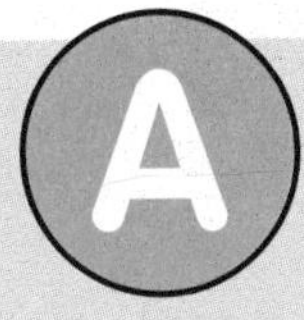

**A** **Put periods after the people's titles in these sentences.**

1. Mr. Forest is our next-door neighbor.
2. Mr and Mrs Forest have a very big garden.
3. Mrs Forest works in her garden on cool mornings.
4. Her friend Dr Maynard stops to visit before work.
5. Mrs Forest gives Dr Maynard some pretty flowers to take to the office.
6. After dinner, Mr Forest likes to weed the garden.
7. Mrs Forest helps him water the plants.

Think of four people who work in your school. Write their names below. Be sure to write Mr., Mrs., Ms., or Dr. before each.

1. ______________________________

2. ______________________________

3. ______________________________

4. ______________________________

Choose two of the people. Write a sentence about each person.

1. ______________________________

______________________________

2. ______________________________

______________________________

Name ______________________________

# Abbreviations for Days and Months

When writing sentences, you should write the full names of the days and the months.

Today is **Tuesday**, **October 9**.

You should also know the **abbreviations** for the names of the days and the months.

Tuesday ➜ **Tues.** October ➜ **Oct.**

**Write the abbreviations for the days and months in the following lists.**

1. Sunday ____________
2. Friday ____________
3. Wednesday ____________
4. Thursday ____________
5. Saturday ____________
6. Monday ____________
7. February ____________
8. March ____________
9. November ____________
10. August ____________
11. September ____________
12. January ____________

*Name* ______________________________

# Post Office Abbreviations

First study the "Post Office State Abbreviations" with a partner, if your teacher says it is okay. Then close your handbook.

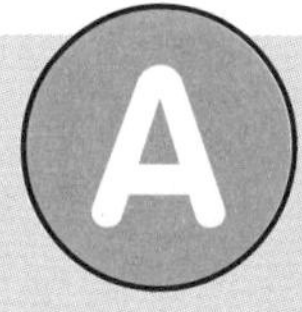


**Draw a line from each state to its post office abbreviation.**

| | |
|---|---|
| **1.** California | CO |
| **2.** Colorado | FL |
| **3.** Florida | KS |
| **4.** Illinois | CA |
| **5.** Kansas | IL |
| **6.** Massachusetts | TX |
| **7.** Michigan | NC |
| **8.** New York | MI |
| **9.** Texas | MA |
| **10.** North Carolina | NY |

*Name* ______________________________

# Checking Mechanics Review 1

This activity reviews some of the ways to use capital letters.

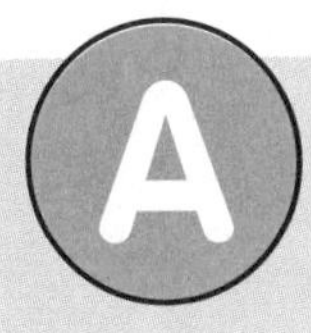

**Put capital letters where they are needed. There are 22 for you to find.**

D
dear tim,

how are you? how is life in florida? today ms. martinez said she wished we could all visit you. i told her i get to visit you in june!

i just read a book called <u>the magic paintbrush</u>. it is a good story from china. lee gave me the book for christmas.

mrs. james said she hopes you like your new school. do you?

Your friend,

roger

**Fill in the blanks below. Use your handbook if you need help.**

1. Write two days of the week that are school days:

   ______________________  ______________________

2. Write the name of a holiday: ______________________
3. Write your first name: ______________________
4. Write the name of a planet: ______________________
5. Write your teacher's name: ______________________

KEEP GOING

**Now use the words you just wrote to complete this story.**

It was ________________ (day of the week), but there was no school. It was ________________ (name of the holiday). ________________ (teacher's name) had a busy day planned. ________________ (your name) was going to build a spaceship and blast off to ________________ (planet).

Name ______________________________

# Checking Mechanics Review 2

This activity reviews plurals and abbreviations.

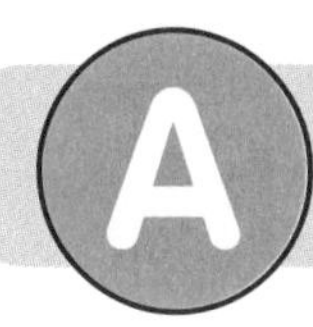

## Write the plural of each animal name.

1. cow ______________
2. donkey ______________
3. finch ______________
4. goose ______________
5. guppy ______________
6. mouse ______________
7. fox ______________
8. pig ______________
9. puppy ______________
10. turkey ______________

## Write the abbreviation for each day of the week.

1. Monday ______________
2. Tuesday ______________
3. Wednesday ______________
4. Thursday ______________
5. Friday ______________
6. Saturday ______________
7. Sunday ______________

**C** **Write the abbreviations for the months of the year.**

1. January ______________________
2. February ______________________
3. March ______________________
4. April ______________________
5. May ______________________
6. June ______________________
7. July ______________________
8. August ______________________
9. September ______________________
10. October ______________________
11. November ______________________
12. December ______________________

*Name* ______________________________

# ABC Order

Words in **alphabetical (ABC) order** are listed by their first letter in the order of the letters of the alphabet.

 apple  banana  cherry  date

**Rewrite this list of names. Put them in alphabetical order.**

| | | |
|---|---|---|
| Ben | **1.** | Adam |
| Ethan | **2.** | |
| Danielle | **3.** | |
| Will | **4.** | |
| Richard | **5.** | |
| Adam | **6.** | |
| Vanessa | **7.** | |
| Isabelle | **8.** | |
| Chris | **9.** | |
| Maria | **10.** | |

Write down the first names of seven students in your class. Each name should begin with a different letter. First write the names in the order you think of them. Then write the names in ABC order.

| Any Order | ABC Order |
|---|---|
| 1. ______ | 1. ______ |
| 2. ______ | 2. ______ |
| 3. ______ | 3. ______ |
| 4. ______ | 4. ______ |
| 5. ______ | 5. ______ |
| 6. ______ | 6. ______ |
| 7. ______ | 7. ______ |

Write a sentence that names one boy and one girl in your class.

______________________________

______________________________

Name ________________________________

# Sorting Nouns

A **noun** names a person, a place, or a thing.

| Person | Place | Thing |
|---|---|---|
| girl | tree house | egg |

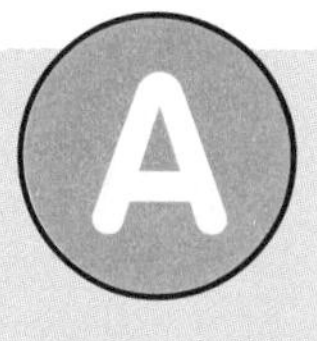

**Sort the words in the box into three groups: words that name people, words that name places, and words that name things.**

| sister | park | computer | zipper | apple | baby |
|---|---|---|---|---|---|
| uncle | table | family | forest | zoo | school |

**People Words**

1. ____________
2. ____________
3. ____________
4. ____________

**Place Words**

1. ____________
2. ____________
3. ____________
4. ____________

**Thing Words**

1. ____________
2. ____________
3. ____________
4. ____________

**B** **Draw a picture that shows one of the place words.**

**Write a sentence or two telling about your picture. Underline the place words.**

*Name* ______________________________

# Sorting Nouns and Verbs

A **noun** names a person, a place, or a thing.

Dalton    mall    cat

A **verb** shows action or helps complete a thought.

throw    are    have

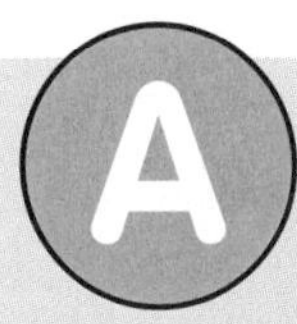

**Sort the words in the box into two groups: nouns and verbs.**

| sun | is | melts | brother | Grand Canyon |
|---|---|---|---|---|
| howled | has | was | Paula | classroom |

| Nouns | Verbs |
|---|---|
| 1. ____________ | 1. ____________ |
| 2. ____________ | 2. ____________ |
| 3. ____________ | 3. ____________ |
| 4. ____________ | 4. ____________ |
| 5. ____________ | 5. ____________ |

Write two sentences. In each sentence, use one noun you listed and one verb you listed.

1. ______________________________

______________________________

2. ______________________________

______________________________

Draw or find a picture to go with one of your sentences.

*Name* ________________________________

# Sorting Long "a" Words and Long "e" Words

A long **a** sound is the vowel sound you hear in **cake, train,** and **day**.

A long **e** sound is the vowel sound you hear in **street, heat,** and **see**.

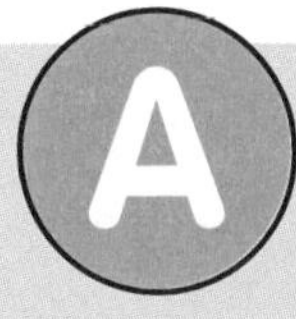

**Sort the words in the box into two groups: words that have the long "a" sound and words that have the long "e" sound.**

| sea | face | beak | snail | bee | snake |
|---|---|---|---|---|---|
| leap | ape | chase | spray | green | chief |

| Long "a" Sound | Long "e" Sound |
|---|---|
| 1. __________ | 1. __________ |
| 2. __________ | 2. __________ |
| 3. __________ | 3. __________ |
| 4. __________ | 4. __________ |
| 5. __________ | 5. __________ |
| 6. __________ | 6. __________ |

**B** Each word pair has either the long "a" sound or the long "e" sound. Write which sound each word pair has.

1. green bee ____________
2. flea feet ____________
3. grape ape ____________
4. whale tail ____________
5. sleepy beast ____________
6. stray snail ____________

Draw a picture that shows one of the word pairs. Then write a silly sentence about your picture.

____________________________________________

Name ______________________________

# Using the Right Word 1

Some words sound alike, but they have different spellings. They also have different meanings. (These words are **homophones.**) Here are some examples:

I hear you. I am here.

## A Fill in each blank with "here" or "hear."

1. I asked my dog Dan to come ___here___ .
2. Can you ______________ what I am saying?
3. Did you ______________ what happened to Sara?
4. ______________ is the ball I thought I lost.
5. I ______________ music.
6. Dan can ______________ better than people.

## B Write a sentence using "hear" and "here."

______________________________________________

______________________________________________

## C

**Read the example sentences using "no" and "know." Then fill in each blank with the correct word.**

Anna said, **"No** thanks."
I **know** about computers.

**1.** There is ________________ more ice cream.

**2.** I ________________ where to get some.

**3.** Just answer yes or ________________ .

**4.** Do you ________________ the new girl?

**5.** I don't ________________ her yet.

**6.** There is ________________ school tomorrow.

## D

**Write a sentence using "no" and "know."**

______________________________________________________

______________________________________________________

Name ______________________________

# Using the Right Word 2

Some words sound alike, but they have different spellings. They also have different meanings. (These words are **homophones**.) Here are some examples:

These shoes are **new**. I **knew** the answer.

**Fill in each blank with "new" or "knew."**

1. I got a ____new____ raincoat.
2. My mom ______________ it was going to rain today.
3. My sister got ______________ boots.
4. Dave wrote a ______________ story.
5. Mike said he ______________ how it would end.
6. We start a ______________ chapter today.

**Write a sentence using "new" and "knew."**

______________________________________________

______________________________________________

**Read the sentence using "sea" and "see." Then fill in each blank with the correct word.**

I would like to **see** a whale in the **sea**.

1. In my dream, I was swimming in the ______________ .
2. I could ________________ under the water.
3. I saw a huge ________________ monster.
4. I could ________________ its big, sharp teeth.
5. I didn't want to ________________ it up close.
6. Now I don't like to swim in the ________________ !

KEEP GOING

**Write a sentence using "sea" and "see."**

______________________________________________

______________________________________________

______________________________________________

Name ______________________

# Using the Right Word 3

Some words sound alike, but they have different spellings. They also have different meanings. (These words are **homophones**.) Here are some examples:

I have **two** cats.
I have a dog, **too**.
I go **to** Pine Elementary.

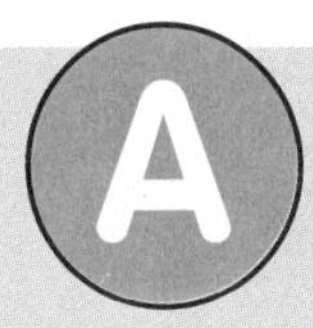

**Fill in each blank with "two," "to," or "too." "Too" can mean "also" or "more than enough."**

1. We are going ____to____ the beach.
2. We can only stay for ____________ hours.
3. Can Marla come, ____________ ?
4. I like to take a radio ____________ the beach.
5. Just don't play it ____________ loud

**Write a sentence using "two" and "to."**

______________________________________________

______________________________________________

## C

**Read the sentence using "read" and "red." Then fill in each blank with the correct word.**

I **read** my **red** notebook.

1. The U.S. flag is ________________ , white, and blue.
2. Our class ________________ about the flag.
3. Candy canes are ________________ and white.
4. Our teacher uses a ________________ pen.
5. Casey ________________ his story to the class.
6. Tina ________________ a poem.

## D

**Write a sentence using "read" and "red."**

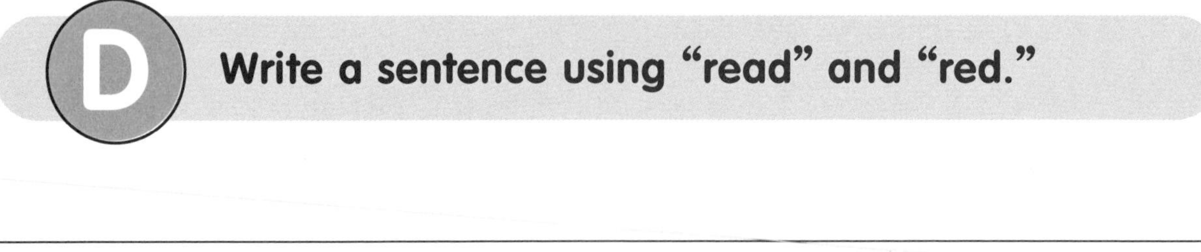

______________________________________________

______________________________________________

Name ________________________________________

# Using the Right Word 4

Some words sound alike, but they have different spellings. They also have different meanings. (These words are **homophones**.) Here are some examples:

We saw **their** new puppy.
("Their" shows ownership.)

**There** are three pets now.

**They're** lots of fun.
(*They're* = they are.)

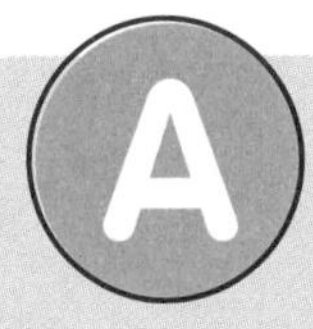


**Fill in each blank with "their," "there," or "they're."**

1. ________________ are four kids in the Clark family.
2. We play freeze tag in ________________ backyard.
3. ________________ my next-door neighbors.
4. ________________ mother loves animals.
5. Sometimes ________________ busy feeding the pets.
6. ________________ are messes to clean up, too!

Write three funny sentences using at least two of these words in each sentence: “their,” “there,” and “they’re.”

1. ______________________________________________

______________________________________________

2. ______________________________________________

______________________________________________

3. ______________________________________________

______________________________________________

Draw a picture for one of your funny sentences.

*Name* ______________________________

# Using the Right Word Review 1

This activity reviews the **homophones** you have practiced.

**Write the correct word in each blank.**

1. Sam took ___two___ (two, to, too) rats ________ (two, to, too) school.

2. The white rat had ________ (read, red) eyes.

3. Someone yelled, "Don't bring them in ________ (hear, here)!"

4. Miss Green said, "I ________ (no, know) what to do."

5. The rats like to sleep in ________ (hear, here).

6. I ________ (no, know) Sam likes his rats.

7. He has a pet spider, ________ (two, to, too).

8. Don has a ________________ pet parrot.
(new, knew)

9. ________________ are more than 300 kinds of parrots.
(Their, There, They're)

10. First he ________________ all about parrots.
(read, red)

11. Then he ________________ how to take care of one.
(new, knew)

12. You should ________________ the parrot talk!
(hear, here)

**B** **Write three sentences. Use one of these words in each sentence: "to," "two," "too."**

1. ____________________________________________

____________________________________________

2. ____________________________________________

____________________________________________

3. ____________________________________________

____________________________________________

*Name* ______________________________

# Using the Right Word Review 2

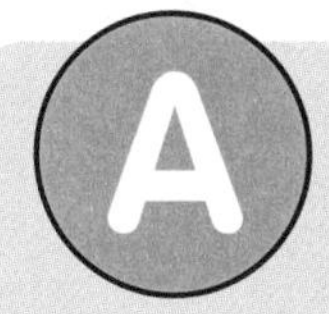


**Before each sentence is a group of words. Choose the correct word to fill in each blank.**

**1. (hear, here)** "Did you ____________ that Uncle Andy and Aunt Sue are coming ____________ ?" I asked.

**2. (know, no)** "Oh, ____________ , I didn't ____________ that," Lea answered.

**3. (read, red)** "They got a little ____________ sailboat," I said. "I ____________ about it in Uncle Andy's letter."

**4. (their, there, they're)** "I hope ____________ bringing ____________ boat when they come," Lea said.

**5. (knew, new)** "Sure," I said. "They ____________ we'd want to sail in the ____________ boat."

**Below are three homophone pairs. Pick one pair, and draw a picture showing those words. (Use your handbook if you need to check meanings.) Then write a sentence about your picture.**

**ant aunt** **ate eight** **dear deer**

# Sentence Activities

This section includes activities related to basic sentence writing, kinds of sentences, and sentence problems.

Name ______________________________

# Understanding Sentences

A **sentence** tells a complete thought.

This is not a complete thought:

On the window.

This is a complete thought:

**A bug is on the window.**

**Check whether each group of words is a complete thought or not.**

| | Complete Thought Yes | Complete Thought No |
|---|---|---|
| **1.** From the downstairs music room. | ______ | ✓ |
| **2.** The sound was very loud. | ______ | ______ |
| **3.** Covered his ears. | ______ | ______ |
| **4.** After that. | ______ | ______ |
| **5.** He shut the front door. | ______ | ______ |
| **6.** Max played the drums. | ______ | ______ |
| **7.** Ming played the piano. | ______ | ______ |
| **8.** Mom the silver flute. | ______ | ______ |

## B Fill in each blank with a word that completes the thought.

1. ________________ was playing with a ball.
2. The ________________ rolled down the hill.
3. ________________ ran after it.
4. Then a big, hairy ________________ ran after it, too.
5. The ________________ got the ball and kept running.
6. Was the ________________ gone for good?

**Draw a picture about sentence 4.**

Name ______________________________

# Parts of a Sentence 1

Every **sentence** has two parts, the **subject** and the **verb**.

Joe planted a seed.

subject ↗ ↖ verb

The subject is the naming part. The verb tells what the subject is doing.

**Underline the subject with one line. Underline the verb with two lines.**

1. Joe watered his seed every day.
2. He watched it carefully.
3. A tiny leaf popped out.
4. The leaf grew larger.
5. A flower bloomed one morning.
6. Joe told his mom.
7. Mom smiled at Joe.
8. Joe gave the flower to his Mom.

## B Write a verb for each sentence.

1. Mom ________________ cookies.
2. I ________________ her.
3. I ________________ the eggs.
4. I ________________ the bowls.
5. Mom ________________ the cookies in the oven.
6. I always ________________ the first cookie.

## C Check whether the underlined word is a subject or a verb.

| | Subject | Verb |
|---|---|---|
| 1. Your body <u>has</u> a lot of bones. | ______ | ______ |
| 2. Your longest <u>bone</u> is in your leg. | ______ | ______ |
| 3. Your ribs <u>look</u> like a cage. | ______ | ______ |
| 4. Your smallest <u>bone</u> is in your ear. | ______ | ______ |
| 5. <u>Jellyfish</u> have no bones. | ______ | ______ |
| 6. A <u>skeleton</u> is all bones. | ______ | ______ |

Name ______________________________

# Parts of a Sentence 2

Every **sentence** has two parts, the **subject** and the **verb**.

Haley came to the party.

**subject** ↗ (Haley) ↖ **verb** (came)

The subject is the naming part. The verb tells what the subject is doing.

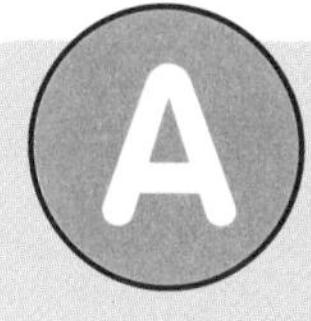


**Fill in each blank with a word from the box. You may use some words more than once.**

| | | | |
|---|---|---|---|
| **Poems** | **Ms. Day** | **Sam** | **Tacos** |
| **Eddy** | **Winter** | **Roses** | **Sarah** |

**1.** ________________ plays on the soccer team.

**2.** Last summer, ________________ drove to Ohio.

**3.** ________________ grow in Grandpa's garden.

**4.** ________________ are my favorite food.

**5.** ________________ sleeps in his doghouse.

**6.** ________________ brings snow and ice to Minnesota.

**Read each sentence in section A again. The word you added is the subject.**

**Fill in each blank with a word from the box. You will use each word only once.**

| learned | barked | is | went |
|---|---|---|---|
| hit | sang | eats | gave |

1. Bobby _______________ a home run.
2. The dog _______________ loudly.
3. Steve _______________ toast every morning.
4. Our teacher _______________ us a test.
5. Kerry _______________ a song for the class.
6. At camp, Cheri _______________ to ride a horse.
7. My sister's name _______________ Gail.
8. We all _______________ for a hike yesterday.

**Read each sentence in section C again. The word you added is the verb.**

Name ______________________________

# Kinds of Sentences 1

A **telling sentence** makes a statement. Put a period after a telling sentence.

**Buster is out in the rain.**

An **asking sentence** asks a question. Put a question mark after an asking sentence.

**Where is Buster?**

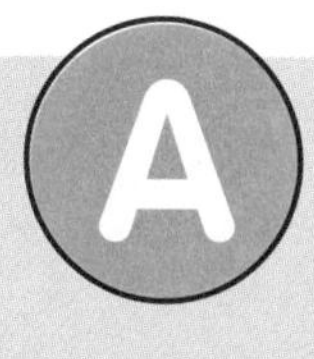



**Write "T" before each telling sentence, and put a period after it. Write "A" before each asking sentence, and put a question mark after it.**

__A__ **1.** What is Sandy doing?

_____ **2.** Sandy is making a bird feeder

_____ **3.** Why is she doing that

_____ **4.** She wants to see what kinds of birds will come

_____ **5.** Where will she put the bird feeder

_____ **6.** She's going to hang it in a tree

_____ **7.** What kind of food will she put in it

_____ **8.** Sandy bought some birdseed for her feeder

## B Draw a picture of some birds at a bird feeder.

Write one telling sentence and one asking sentence about your picture.

1. Telling Sentence: ______________________________

2. Asking Sentence: ______________________________

Name ______________________________

# Kinds of Sentences 2

A **telling sentence** makes a statement. Put a period after a telling sentence.

I'll feed Buster.

An **asking sentence** asks a question. Put a question mark after an asking sentence.

Would you feed Buster, please?

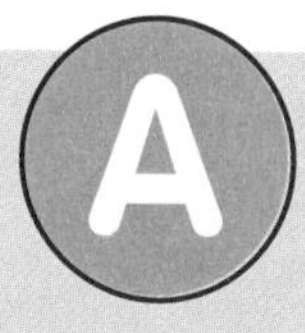

**Write a telling sentence that is an answer for each asking sentence. Make sure you write complete sentences.**

1. What happened to your shoes?

______________________________

2. Who left the door open?

______________________________

3. How did you get all muddy?

______________________________

4. Have you read Too Many Tamales?

______________________________

Pretend that you are only four years old. Write some asking sentences that a four-year-old might ask. Two examples have been done for you.

1. Where do bugs come from?
2. Why does it get dark at night?
3. ______
4. ______
5. ______

Pick two questions from above. Write telling sentences to answer them. (Write interesting answers that are complete sentences!)

1. ______

______

2. ______

______

Name ______________________________

# Sentence Review

This reviews what you have learned about sentences.

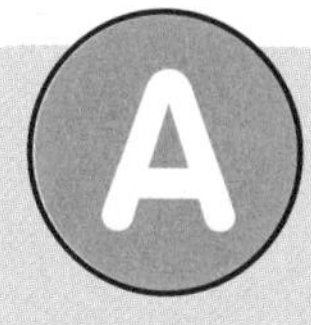

**Write "S" after each sentence. Write "X" after each group of words that is not a sentence.**

1. My dad and I. ______
2. Went to Blue Hills Park. ______
3. We hiked to the top of a big hill. ______
4. Above the clouds! ______
5. Then Treasure Cave. ______
6. It was scary and dark inside. ______
7. Later, we saw three fat raccoons. ______
8. We had a lot of fun. ______
9. Will visit the park again. ______

**Read page 62 in your handbook to see how the writer made each group of words a complete thought.**

**Underline and label the subjects and verbs in the sentences that begin with "I." The first sentence has been done for you.**

Dear Grandma,

Guess what? I (S) lost (V) another tooth! I bit into an apple. I feel the new hole in my mouth now.

Mom will bring me to your house next week. I like your yard. I think your new slide is great!

Will you bake cookies for me? See you soon.

Love,

John

**Copy one asking sentence and one telling sentence from the letter.**

**1.** Asking Sentence: ______________________

______________________

**2.** Telling Sentence: ______________________

______________________

# Language Activities

The activities in this section are related to the parts of speech. All of the activities have a page link to *Write Away*. In addition, KEEP GOING, which is at the end of many activities, encourages follow-up practice of certain skills.

Name ______________________________

# Nouns

A **noun** names a person, a place, or a thing.

| Person | Place | Thing |
|---|---|---|
| student | park | cake |
| friend | mall | candle |

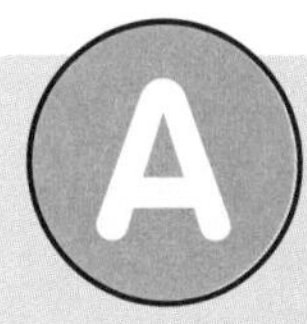

**Write what each noun is: "person," "place," or "thing." Add three nouns of your own.**

1. firefighter ______person______
2. library ____________________
3. hammer ____________________
4. teacher ____________________
5. pencil ____________________
6. store ____________________
7. __________ ____________________
8. __________ ____________________
9. __________ ____________________

Write "N" if the word is a noun. Write "X" if the word is not a noun.

_____ 1. paper _____ 4. bring _____ 7. and

_____ 2. go _____ 5. girl _____ 8. hot

_____ 3. bee _____ 6. store _____ 9. kite

Underline the noun in each sentence.

1. The bus is yellow.
2. The spider jumped.
3. This game is hard.
4. Look at the duck!
5. The sky looks pretty.
6. A friend called.

Write a sentence about your favorite toys. Then underline the nouns in your sentence.

_______________________________________________

_______________________________________________

_______________________________________________

Name ______________________________

# Singular and Plural Nouns

**Singular** means one.

elephant

**Plural** means more than one.

elephant**s**

Plural nouns usually end with **"s."**

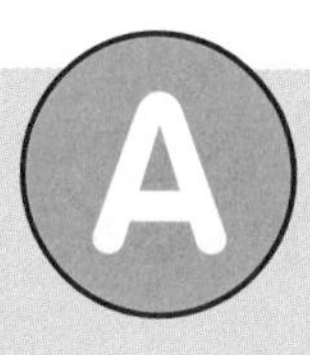

**Write "S" if the noun is singular. Write "P" if the noun is plural.**

__P__ **1.** boxes

_____ **2.** table

_____ **3.** chairs

_____ **4.** rug

_____ **5.** truck

_____ **6.** toys

**Write "S" if the underlined noun is singular. Write "P" if the underlined noun is plural.**

_____ **1.** I like <u>art</u>.

_____ **2.** I have <u>crayons</u>.

_____ **3.** <u>Paints</u> are messy.

_____ **4.** It's for my <u>sister</u>.

Underline the plural noun in each sentence.

1. The cow has black and white spots.
2. Some piglets are pink.
3. Potatoes spilled out of the grocery bag.
4. My sister baked chocolate chip cookies yesterday.
5. Tony took off his muddy shoes.
6. Erin held the tiny kittens.

Draw a picture about one of the plural nouns you underlined. Write the noun under your picture.

*Name* ______________________

# Common and Proper Nouns 1

A **common noun** tells what a thing is. A **proper noun** tells a thing's name.

| Common Noun | Proper Noun |
|---|---|
| boy | Tony Prada |
| school | Hill Elementary |
| city | Lexington |

A proper noun begins with a capital letter. Some proper nouns are more than one word.

**Underline the common noun in each sentence.**

1. The class is busy writing.
2. The teacher likes to help.
3. The girl is reading quietly.
4. The street is shiny and wet.
5. The sandy beach is hot.
6. Let's swim in the pool!
7. My puppy is furry and brown.
8. He has a red collar.

Underline the proper noun in each sentence.

1. We stopped at Jefferson Library.
2. Susie wanted a book about horses.
3. This book is about President Lincoln.
4. Principal Brown visited the library.
5. He speaks Spanish.
6. Rosa Perez does, too.

Write "C" if the underlined word is a common noun. Write "P" if the underlined word is a proper noun.

_____ 1. My neighbor walks her dog each afternoon.

_____ 2. My neighbor's name is Mrs. Lee.

_____ 3. Her dog likes me.

_____ 4. Alf is a funny dog.

_____ 5. One day he got on a bus.

_____ 6. The bus driver said, "No dogs on the bus!"

Name ______________________________

# Common and Proper Nouns 2

A **common noun** tells what a thing is. A **proper noun** tells a thing's name.

| Common Noun | Proper Noun |
|---|---|
| holiday | New Year's Day |
| country | Mexico |

A proper noun begins with a capital letter. Some proper nouns are more than one word.

**Write "C" if the word is a common noun. Write "P" if the word is a proper noun.**

__C__ **1.** cat

_____ **2.** Sun Park

_____ **3.** library

_____ **4.** Washington, D.C.

_____ **5.** flag

_____ **6.** Jennifer

_____ **7.** Main Street

_____ **8.** book

_____ **9.** mountain

_____ **10.** Rocky Mountains

**Draw a line from each common noun to the proper noun that fits with it.**

| | |
|---|---|
| **1.** girl | United States |
| **2.** boy | Fluffy |
| **3.** cat | "The Three Bears" |
| **4.** country | Tom |
| **5.** story | Lisa |

**Write "C" if the underlined noun is a common noun. Write "P" if the underlined noun is a proper noun.**

_____ **1.** Today is Christmas!

_____ **2.** There is no school today.

_____ **3.** The air is freezing cold.

_____ **4.** Aunt Lizzie visited us.

_____ **5.** Kevin brought ribbon candy.

_____ **6.** He is from Korea.

Name ______________________________

# Possessive Nouns

A **possessive noun** shows ownership. A possessive noun has an **apostrophe**.

Tia's toy boat was left out in the yard.
(The toy boat belongs to Tia.)

After the storm, we found it in the dog's house.
(The house belongs to the dog.)

A **Circle the possessive nouns.**

1. Mike's story about Mr. Bug was fun to read.
2. Mr. Bug's house was flooded when it rained.
3. When a toy boat floated by, Mr. Bug's 148 children hopped in.
4. All the little Bugs waited for the storm's end.
5. Finally the boat floated to a dog's house.
6. The dog's name was Buddy.
7. The little Bugs asked if they could share their new friend's home.
8. The story's title is "The Bugs Find a Buddy."

Draw a picture of one of these things from the story:

* Bug's flooded house,
* the child's toy boat, or
* the dog's house.

Write a sentence telling about your picture. Use a possessive noun. (Remember to use an apostrophe.)

*Name* ______________________________________

# Pronouns 1

A **pronoun** is a word that takes the place of a noun.

| Noun | Pronoun |
|---|---|
| **Todd** did it. | **He** did it. |
| **Sally** laughed. | **She** laughed. |
| The **rope** broke. | **It** broke. |
| The **skates** are too big. | **They** are too big. |

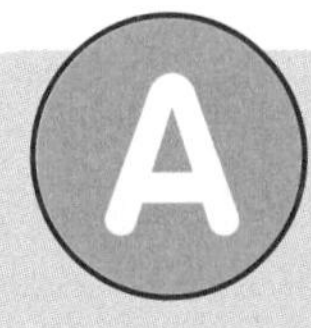

**Circle the pronouns that replace the underlined nouns in the sentences below.**

1. Holly gave Katy a Mexican coin.

   She gave Katy a Mexican coin.

2. Katy put the coin in a safe place.

   Katy put it in a safe place.

3. Peggy and Jo wanted to see the coin.

   They wanted to see the coin.

4. Then Jay asked to see it, too.

   Then he asked to see it, too.

**B** Draw a line from each noun to the pronoun that could replace it.

| | |
|---|---|
| 1. Dad and Mom | he |
| 2. the girl | it |
| 3. Grandpa | I |
| 4. the TV | we |
| 5. Shari and I | they |
| 6. ________________ (write your first name here) | she |

**C** In each sentence, write a pronoun to replace the noun. If you need help, check the list of pronouns on page 280 in your handbook.

1. ________________ went to a movie.
   (Jim and Ray)

2. ________________ broke his arm.
   (The boy)

3. A doctor fixed ________________ .
   (the arm)

4. ________________ is a good writer.
   (Jane)

*Name* ____________________________________

# Pronouns 2

A **pronoun** can take the place of a possessive noun. A possessive noun shows ownership.

| Noun | Pronoun |
| --- | --- |
| Jan's bicycle | her bicycle |
| Dave's skateboard | his skateboard |
| the bird's wing | its wing |
| Mike and Laura's poem | their poem |

**Circle the pronouns that take the place of the underlined nouns in the sentences below.**

1. Juanita's coat is hanging up.

   Her coat is hanging up.

2. At the picnic, Jake's lunch fell into the water.

   At the picnic, his lunch fell into the water.

3. Yesterday Sam and Sarah's bus left early.

   Yesterday their bus left early.

4. The dog was very excited.

   It chewed on a big bone.

Underline the pronoun in each sentence. Draw a picture of the pet rat.

1. Here is my pet rat.
2. Dad likes its pink ears.
3. Mom likes its long tail.
4. Bogart is our favorite pet.
5. He has red eyes.
6. Ted pets his white fur.
7. We bought a blue cage.

Draw a line to the pronoun that could replace the underlined words.

| | |
|---|---|
| 1. I heard Tim and Judy's song. | ours |
| 2. I know your sister's name. | Its |
| 3. Here comes Ricky's friend. | their |
| 4. The book's cover got wet. | his |
| 5. The tree house is yours and mine. | her |

Name ______________________________

# Pronouns 3

A **pronoun** is a word that takes the place of a noun.

Jason made a sandwich.
Then he ate it.
(The pronouns “he” and “it” take the place of the nouns “Jason” and “sandwich.”)

**Fill in each blank with a pronoun that replaces the underlined word or words.**

1. Joe and Ann read a poem. ____They____ read it aloud.
2. Tanya drew a map. ________ showed it to me.
3. My brother and I have a clubhouse. ________ made it ourselves.
4. I hope you’re coming to my party. ________ will be fun.
5. Mom heard our music. ________ was too loud.
6. Tony is coming over. ________ is my friend.
7. The monkeys at the zoo played baseball. ________ were funny.
8. This book is great. ________ has good pictures, too.

## B Use each pronoun in a sentence.

| I | we | she | they |
|---|---|---|---|

1. ______________________________

2. ______________________________

3. ______________________________

4. ______________________________

## C Draw a picture to go with one of your sentences.

*Name* ______________________________

# Action Verbs

There are different kinds of **verbs**. Some verbs show action:

Mom **found** our jump rope.
She **gave** it to us.

**Underline the action verb in each sentence.**

1. Al brings the rope.
2. Eli and Linda hold the rope.
3. They twirl the rope.
4. The other kids count for Al.
5. Scott's dog Stripe barks at Al.
6. Sometimes Al jumps 100 times!
7. Then Linda takes a turn.
8. Mother waves from the window.
9. She points at Stripe.
10. The kids laugh.

## B Here are some more action verbs. Fill in each blank with a verb from this box.

| | | |
|---|---|---|
| dive | point | pop |
| roars | visit | eat |

1. Paul and Ann ____________________ the zoo.
2. They ____________________ at some lions.
3. One of the lions ____________________ at them.
4. The elephants ____________________ lots of peanuts.
5. The polar bears ____________________ into the pool.
6. Prairie dogs ____________________ out of their tunnels.

**Write a sentence about the zoo. Use an action verb.**

______________________________________________________________

______________________________________________________________

______________________________________________________________

Name ______________________________

# Action and Linking Verbs

**Action verbs** show action. Here are some examples:

kick tell throw ask run write

**Linking verbs** complete a thought or an idea. Here are some examples:

am was is were are be

**Write "A" if the underlined verb is an action verb. Write "L" if the verb is a linking verb.**

A **1.** Soccer players kick the ball.

____ **2.** Football players throw the ball.

____ **3.** I am cold.

____ **4.** Pat and Rob run around the track.

____ **5.** She is a fast runner

____ **6.** They are both in second grade.

____ **7.** He paints pictures.

____ **8.** Pete and Joni were sick.

Pick five action verbs from the list on page 283 in your handbook. Use each action verb in a sentence.

1. ______________________________________________

______________________________________________

2. ______________________________________________

______________________________________________

3. ______________________________________________

______________________________________________

4. ______________________________________________

______________________________________________

5. ______________________________________________

______________________________________________

Write a sentence using the linking verb "am."

______________________________________________

______________________________________________

Name ______________________________

# Verbs: Present and Past Tense

A verb that tells what is happening now is called a **present-tense verb.**

Sean is in second grade.
He takes swimming lessons every week.

A verb that tells what happened in the past is called a **past-tense verb.**

Last year he was in first grade.
He learned to play soccer.

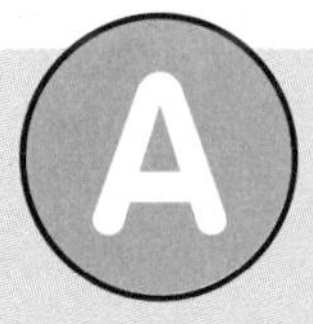

**Check whether each underlined verb is in the present tense or the past tense.**

| | Present Tense | Past Tense |
|---|---|---|
| **1.** Bobby broke his leg last weekend. | ______ | ✓ |
| **2.** He fell out of a big tree. | ______ | ______ |
| **3.** Now he has a cast on his leg. | ______ | ______ |
| **4.** He is home from school this week. | ______ | ______ |
| **5.** Yesterday I took him his homework. | ______ | ______ |
| **6.** I wrote my name on his cast. | ______ | ______ |
| **7.** Bobby walks with crutches. | ______ | ______ |

**Complete the following sentences. Write the present-tense verb or the past-tense verb in the blank. The first one has been done for you.**

**Present Tense**

1. Now Mom makes my lunches for school. (makes, made)
2. Now I ______________ eight years old. (am, was)
3. The sidewalk ______________ slippery when it snows. (gets, got)
4. Now Stanis ______________ swimming lessons. (takes, took)

**Past Tense**

1. Last week I ______________ to school with Hector. (walk, walked)
2. Yesterday Lydia ______________ a letter to her aunt. (write, wrote)
3. Last summer our family ______________ camping. (goes, went)
4. This morning I ______________ late for school. (am, was)

Name ______________________________

# Adjectives 1

An **adjective** describes a noun or a pronoun. An adjective often comes before the word it describes.

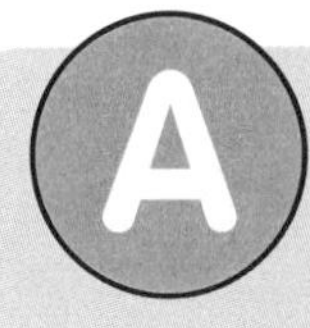

Megan has **long** hair.
Randy wears a **black** cap.

Sometimes an **adjective** comes after the word it describes.

Parrots are **colorful**.

**A** **Underline the adjective that describes each circled noun.**

1. Elephants are huge animals.
2. Their skin is wrinkled.
3. Their ivory tusks are long teeth.
4. Elephants use their floppy ears as giant fans.
5. An elephant's trunk works as a useful tool.
6. It can pick up small peanuts.
7. A cool river is an elephant's favorite place.

Fill in each blank with an adjective that describes the circled noun.

1. Elephants make ________________ noises.
2. Elephants have ________________ trunks.
3. They have ________________ feet.
4. Elephants can carry ________________ loads.
5. Would you take a ________________ ride on an elephant?
6. How would you get on a ________________ elephant?

Underline each adjective that describes the circled pronoun.

1. You are smart.
2. He is funny.
3. They look tired.
4. I am hungry.
5. It is green.
6. We are cold.
7. She feels sick.
8. They taste stale.

*Name* ______________________________

# Adjectives 2

An **adjective** describes a noun or a pronoun. An adjective often comes before the word it describes.

The **hungry** bear sniffed the berries.

Sometimes an **adjective** comes after the word it describes.

The bear was **hungry**.

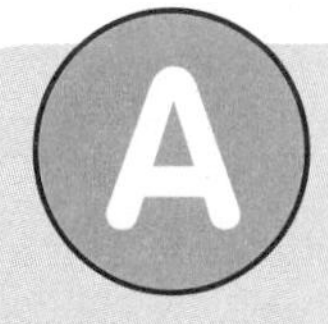

**Underline the adjectives in this song. There are 19 in all. (Don't underline "a" or "that.")**

I'm going to tell you a story about a grizzly bear.

It's just a little story about a grizzly bear.

It was a great big, grizzly, grizzly bear.

a great big, grizzly, grizzly bear.

Mama ran away from that grizzly bear.

So daddy went a-hunting for that grizzly bear.

He had long, long hair that grizzly bear.

He had big blue eyes that grizzly bear.

Write one more sentence for "The Grizzly Bear Song." Underline the adjectives you use.

______________________________________________

______________________________________________

Write two sentences using adjectives from the box below. Try using more than one adjective in your sentences.

| hairy | purple | loud | cold |
|---|---|---|---|
| dizzy | smelly | squeaky | soft |
| windy | wet | sweet | sour |
| chewy | sleepy | strong | goofy |

1. ______________________________________________

______________________________________________

2. ______________________________________________

______________________________________________

Name ______________________________

# Articles

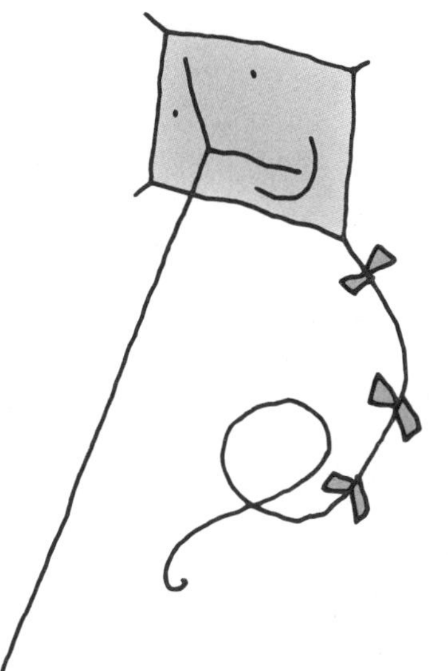

The words **"a," "an,"** and **"the"** are **articles.**

Use **"a"** before a consonant sound.

a kite

Use **"an"** before a vowel sound.

an ocean

## A Write "a" or "an" before the following words.

| | |
|---|---|
| ___an___ **1.** attic | ________ **10.** whale |
| ________ **2.** chicken | ________ **11.** shadow |
| ________ **3.** shovel | ________ **12.** envelope |
| ________ **4.** elephant | ________ **13.** idea |
| ________ **5.** tooth | ________ **14.** monkey |
| ________ **6.** giant | ________ **15.** orange |
| ________ **7.** dinosaur | ________ **16.** package |
| ________ **8.** apple | ________ **17.** kettle |
| ________ **9.** spider | ________ **18.** inchworm |

## B Fill in the word "a" or "an" in the spaces below.

One day ________ spider with yellow feet climbed to the top of ________ slide. The slide was in ________ park. Soon the spider heard ________ radio playing her favorite song. The song was ________ old tune called "The Eensy Weensy Spider." The spider began to tap her eight yellow feet. ________ inchworm heard the music, too. He inched his way over to the slide and began to tap all of his feet. What ________ funny sight to see! ________ spider and ________ inchworm were dancing in the park.

**Draw a picture of the spider and the inchworm.**

Name ___________________________

# Parts of Speech Review 1

This activity is a review of the parts of speech you have practiced: **nouns (N), pronouns (P), verbs (V),** and **adjectives (A).**

**What part of speech is underlined in each sentence? Write "N," "P," "V," or "A" in the blank.**

__A__ **1.** A toasted cheese sandwich is great.

_____ **2.** It smells buttery and looks golden brown.

_____ **3.** When I bite into it, I see the melted cheese.

_____ **4.** Toasted cheese sandwiches taste crunchy on the outside and creamy in the middle.

_____ **5.** My mom makes them on the griddle.

_____ **6.** I could eat one every day!

_____ **7.** I hope we have toasted cheese sandwiches for dinner tonight.

_____ **8.** It would be a super way to end my day.

## B Fill in the blanks below.

**1.** Write the name of your favorite food (noun):

______________________________________________

**2.** Write a word that describes it (adjective):

______________________________________________

## C Fill in each blank with a word that is the correct part of speech.

**1.** ______________ likes tuna sandwiches.
(noun)

**2.** ______________ like tacos better.
(pronoun)

**3.** I ______________ two tacos every day.
(verb)

**4.** I like them with ______________ cheese.
(adjective)

**5.** Sandra's mom ______________ the best tacos.
(verb)

**6.** She puts ______________ sauce on them.
(adjective)

Name ______________________________

# Parts of Speech Review 2

Do this activity with a partner. (It's about sushi, a special Japanese cold rice cake.)

**Label all the nouns "N" and the pronouns "P."**

1. Yesterday Mom and I went to the Japanese grocery store.
2. We bought raw tuna and salmon.
3. This morning Mom cooked the rice.
4. With a flat spoon, I spread it on the seaweed.
5. We can add avocados and mushrooms, too.

**Label all the verbs "V" and the adjectives "A."**

1. We added orange carrots and green spinach.
2. As I rolled it together, I squeezed the yummy sushi.
3. With a sharp knife, Mom cut the roll into small pieces.
4. Then we poured dipping sauce into tiny bowls.
5. We also ate thin slices of pickled ginger.

**C** Think of a song or poem you know. Write down at least four lines from it. (You could use a poem you wrote, or one from your handbook.)

In the lines above, find and label two nouns and two verbs. Also label any pronouns and adjectives.

Name ____________________

# Theme Words

Lists of **theme words** can help you choose and spell interesting words for your writing.

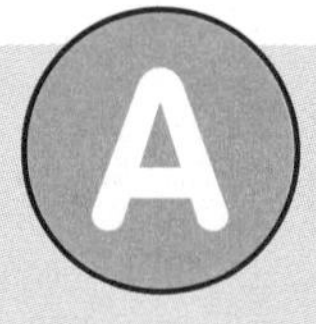

**Think of a favorite topic. Then list your own theme words below.**

Topic: ____________________

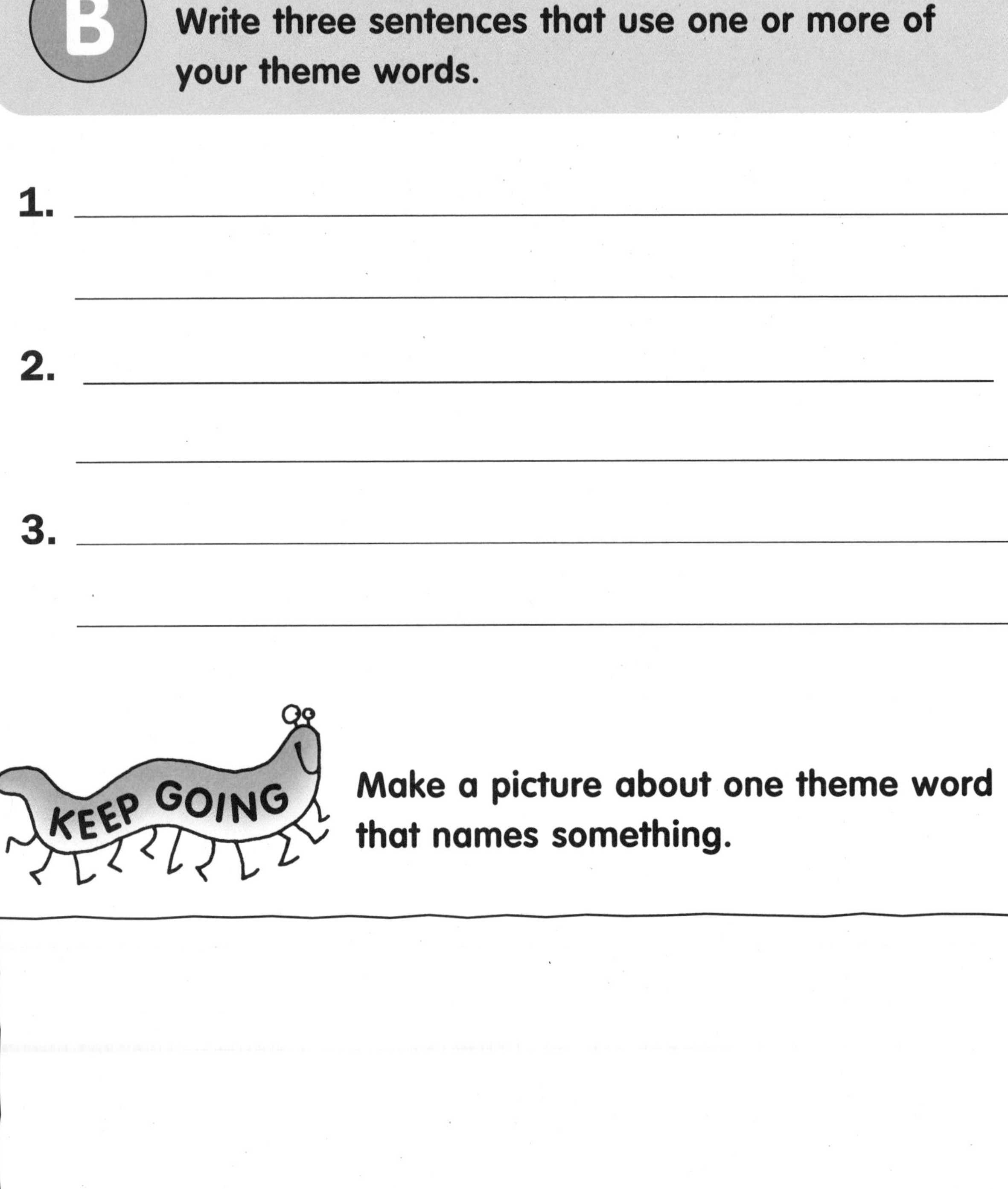


**B** Write three sentences that use one or more of your theme words.

1. ______________________________

______________________________

2. ______________________________

______________________________

3. ______________________________

______________________________

**KEEP GOING** Make a picture about one theme word that names something.